ELIJAH

ELIJAH:

AND THE SECRET OF HIS POWER

F. B. Meyer

CHRISTIAN LITERATURE CRUSADE
Fort Washington, Pennsylvania 19034

CHRISTIAN LITERATURE CRUSADE
Fort Washington, Pennsylvania 19034

CANADA
1757 Avenue Road, Toronto, Ontario M5M 3Y8

Originally published by
Fleming H. Revell Co.

Published in the United Kingdom by
Marshall, Morgan & Scott Ltd.

This American edition 1978
under special arrangement with
the British publisher.

SBN 87508-343-9

PREFACE TO THE ORIGINAL EDITION

THESE chapters were first delivered as a series of sermons to my beloved people at Melbourne Hall; and then transcribed for *The Christian*, from the pages of which they are now reprinted, in answer to many requests.

Some of my readers may be disposed to charge me with rashness in attempting to delineate the life of Elijah—this Colossus amongst ordinary men; who dwarfs us, whilst his own noble proportions defy the belittling perspective of long distance. But my excuse will be found in the thought, reiterated on many a succeeding page, that the life of this mighty man was wrought out through the indwelling of that Holy Spirit, which is equally within reach of those who will believe and obey.

There is nothing the Church of to-day needs so much as Spiritual Power; and there is nothing which we can have so easily, if only we are prepared to pay the price.

It is of no use to exclaim, in despairing tones, "Where is the Lord God of Elijah?" He is here, waiting to do as much now as for the illustrious saints of olden times. Be it ours to emulate their faith; and to stand as they did in the presence-chamber of God, prepared to fulfil His least behest: so shall we be followers of them who, through faith and patience, inherit the promises.

F. B. MEYER.

CONTENTS

I

THE SOURCE OF ELIJAH'S STRENGTH
(1 KINGS XVII)

THIS chapter begins with the conjunction "And": it is, therefore, an addition to what has gone before; and it is *God's* addition. When we have read to the end of the previous chapter—which tells the melancholy story of the rapid spread, and universal prevalence, of idolatry, in the favoured land of the Ten Tribes—we might suppose that that was the end of all; and that the worship of Jehovah would never again acquire its lost prestige and power. And, no doubt, the principal actors in the story thought so too. Ahab thought so; Jezebel thought so; the false prophets thought so; the scattered remnant of hidden disciples thought so.

But they had made an unfortunate omission in their calculations—they had left out Jehovah Himself. He must have something to say at such a crisis. He must add a few chapters before the history is closed. When men have done their worst, and finished, it is the time for God to begin. And when God begins, He is likely, with one blow, to reverse all that has been done without Him; and to write some pages of human history, which will be a lesson and an inspiration to all coming time.

That "And" is ominous enough to His foes; but it is full of hope and promise to His friends.

Things were dark enough. After the death of Solomon, his kingdom split into two parts—the southern under Rehoboam his son; the northern under Jeroboam, who

9

had superintended the vast public works. Jeroboam was desperately eager to keep his hold on his people; but he feared to lose it, if they continued to go, two or three times in the year, to the annual feasts at Jerusalem. He thought that old associations might overpower their new-born loyalty to himself. He resolved, therefore, to set up the worship of Jehovah in his own territories; and erected two temples, one at Dan, in the extreme north, the other at Bethel, in the extreme south. And in each of these he placed a golden calf; that the God of Israel might be worshipped "under the form of a calf that eateth hay." This sin broke the second commandment—which forbade the children of Israel to make any graven image; or to bow down before the likeness of anything in heaven above, or in the earth beneath. So weak and sinful a bid for popularity is never forgotten in Holy Scripture. Like a funeral knell, the words ring out again and again: "Jeroboam, the son of Nebat, who made Israel to sin."

After many revolutions, and much bloodshed, the kingdom passed into the hands of a military adventurer, Omri. The son of this man was Ahab, of whom it is said, "he did more to provoke the Lord God of Israel to anger than all the kings of Israel that were before him." This came to pass, not so much because his character was more depraved: but because he was a weak man, the tool of a crafty, unscrupulous, and cruel woman: and some of the worst crimes that have ever been committed have been wrought by weak men, at the instigation of worse—but stronger—spirits than themselves.

When the young and beautiful Jezebel left the ceiled palaces of Tyre, to become the consort of the newly-crowned king of Israel, it was no doubt regarded as a splendid match. Tyre at that time sat as queen upon the seas, in the zenith of her glory: her colonies dotted the shores of the Mediterranean as far as Spain; her ships whitened every sea with their sails, and ventured to the coasts of our own Cornwall for tin; her daughter, Carthage, nursed the lion-cub Hannibal, and was strong enough to make Rome tremble. But, like many a splendid match, it was fraught with misery and disaster. No one can disobey God's plain words against intermarriage with the ungodly without suffering for it at last.

As she left her palace-home, Jezebel would be vehemently urged by the priests—beneath whose influence she had been trained, and who, therefore, exercised an irresistible spell over her—to do her utmost to introduce into Israel the hideous and cruel rites of her hereditary religion. Nor was she slow to obey. First, she seems to have erected a temple to Astarte in the neighbourhood of Jezreel, the Windsor of the land; and to have supported its four hundred and fifty priests from the revenues of her private purse. Then Ahab and she built a temple for Baal in Samaria, the capital of the kingdom, large enough to contain immense crowds of worshippers (2 Kings x. 21). Shrines and temples then began to rise in all parts of the land in honour of these false deities; whilst the altars of Jehovah, like that at Carmel, were ruthlessly broken down. The land swarmed with the priests of Baal and of the groves—proud of Court favour; glorying in their sudden rise to power; insolent, greedy, licentious, and debased. The fires of persecution were lit, and began to burn with fury. The schools of the prophets were shut up; grass grew in their courts. The prophets themselves were hunted down, and slain by the sword. "They wandered about in sheepskins and goatskins, being destitute, afflicted, tormented;" so much so, that the pious Obadiah had the greatest difficulty in saving a few of them, by hiding them in the limestone caves of Carmel, and feeding them at the risk of his own life.

The whole land seemed apostate. Of all the thousands of Israel, only seven thousand remained who had not bowed the knee or kissed the hand to Baal. But they were paralysed with fear; and kept so still, that their very existence was unknown by Elijah in the hour of his greatest loneliness. Such times have often come, fraught with woe: false religions have gained the upper hand; iniquity has abounded; and the love of many has waxed cold. So was it when the Turk swept over the Christian communities of Asia Minor, and replaced the Cross by the crescent. So was it when, over Europe, Roman Catholicism spread as a pall of darkness that grew denser as the dawn of the Reformation was on the point of breaking. So was it in the last century, when Moderatism reigned in Scotland, and apathy in England.

But God is never at a loss. The land may be overrun with sin; the lamps of witness may seem all extinguished; the whole force of the popular current may run counter to His truth; and the plot may threaten to be within a hair's breadth of entire success; but, all the time, He will be preparing a weak man in some obscure highland village; and in the moment of greatest need will send him forth, as His all-sufficient answer to the worst plottings of His foes. "When the enemy shall come in like a flood, the Spirit of the Lord shall lift up a standard against him." So it has been; and so it shall be again.

Elijah was of the inhabitants of Gilead. Gilead lay east of the Jordan; it was wild and rugged; its hills were covered with shaggy forests; its awful solitudes were only broken by the dash of mountain streams; its valleys were the haunt of fierce wild beasts. "What the highlands of

Argyleshire and Inverness were a century ago to the low-land towns of Scotland, that must Gilead have been to the more refined and civilized people of Jerusalem and Samaria." The inhabitants of Gilead partook of the character of their country—wild, lawless, and unkempt. They dwelt in rude stone villages; and subsisted by keeping flocks of sheep.

Elijah grew up like the other lads of his age. In his early years he would probably do the work of a shepherd on those wild hills. As he grew to manhood, his erect figure, his shaggy locks, his cloak of camel's hair, his muscular, sinewy strength—which could outstrip the fiery coursers of the royal chariot, and endure excessive physical fatigue—distinguished him from the dwellers in lowland valleys; but in none of these would he be specially different from the men who grew up with him in the obscure mountain hamlet of Thisbe, whence he derived the name of Tishbite. There were many amongst them as lithe, and swift, and strong, and capable of fatigue, as he. We must not look to these things for the secret of his strength.

As he grew in years, he became characterized by an intense religious earnestness. He was "very jealous for the Lord God of hosts." Deeply taught in Scripture, especially in those passages which told how much Jehovah had done for his people, Elijah yearned, with passionate desire, that they should give Him His meed of honour. And when he learnt that this was lacking—as the dread tidings came, by broken snatches, of what was transpiring across the Jordan; as messenger after messenger told how Jezebel had thrown down God's altars, and slain His prophets, and replaced them by the impious rites of her Tyrian deities—his blood ran liquid fire; his indignation burst all bounds; he was "very jealous for the Lord God of hosts." O noble heart! would that we could be as righteously indignant, amid the evils of our time ! Oh for a coal from that pure flame that burnt on thine inner hearth !

But the question was, How should he act ? What could he do, a wild, untutored child of the desert ? There was only one thing he could do—the resource of all much-tried souls—he could pray; and he did: "he prayed earnestly" (James v. 17). And in his prayer he seems to have been led back to a denunciation made, years before, by Moses to the people—that if they turned aside, and served other gods and worshipped them, the Lord's wrath would be kindled against them; and He would shut up the heaven, that there should be no rain (Deut. xi. 17). Flowing into this mould, his thoughts must have shaped themselves somewhat thus: "If my God does not fulfil this threat, the people will think that it is an idle tale; or that He is a myth of the past, a dead tradition. This must not be. Better far that the land should suffer the terrors of famine; and the people experience the bitterest agonies of thirst; and that I should be torn limb from limb. It were better that we should suffer the direst physical woes that can blast our national prosperity, than that we should come to think that the Jehovah of our fathers is as dead as the idols of the heathen." And so he set himself to pray that the terrible threat might be literally fulfilled. "He prayed earnestly that it might not rain."

A terrible prayer indeed ! Granted; and yet, was it not more terrible for the people to forget and ignore the God of their fathers, and to give themselves up to the licentious orgies of Baal and Astarte ? Remember, too, what a wrong construction might be put upon the utter silence of God Himself. Could anything be more disastrous than that the statute-book should be filled with laws which the Lawgiver could not, or would not, enforce ? Nothing could be more detrimental to the true conception of God.

"These things hast thou done, and I kept silence; thou
thoughtest that I was altogether such an one as thyself: but I
will reprove thee, and set them in order before thine eyes."

Physical suffering is a smaller calamity than moral
delinquency. And the love of God does not shrink from
inflicting such suffering, if, as a result, the plague of sin may
be cut out as a cancer, and stayed. It may be, reader, that
this is why there is so much sorrow in thy life. Thou art
suffering a terrible drought, before which all the springs of
thy prosperity are drying up. No dews of grace or rains of
blessing have fallen to thy lot for many days. This is not
a chance; it is the work of One who loves thee too well to
permit thee to forsake Himself without making one effort
to arrest and change thee. The cornfield is fired only
because He wants to bring thee to Himself (2 Sam. xiv. 30).
The drought is sent only to enforce the rebuilding of the
altar on Carmel's height, and the immolation of the false
priests in the vale beneath.

And as Elijah prayed, the conviction was wrought into
his mind that it should be even as he prayed; and that he
should go to acquaint Ahab with the fact. Whatever might
be the hazard to himself, both king and people must be
made to connect their calamities with the true cause. And
this they evidently did, as we shall see (i Kings xviii. 10).
That the drought was due to his prayer is also to be inferred
from the express words with which Elijah announced the
fact to the king: "There shall not be dew nor rain these
years, *but according to my word.*"

What a meeting was that ! We know not where it took
place; whether in the summer palace, when Jezebel was at
her consort's side, or when Ahab was surrounded by his
high officers of state in Samaria. But wherever it took
place, it was a subject worthy of the highest art and genius.
The old religion against the new; the child of nature

against the effeminate child of courts; camel's hair against soft clothing; moral strength against moral weakness.

This interview needed no ordinary moral strength. It was no child's play for the untutored child of the desert to go on such an errand to that splendid court ! What chance was there of his escaping with his life ? Surely he would not fare better than the prophets, who had not dared so much as he ! Yet he went and came unhurt, in the panoply of a might which seemed invulnerable.

What was the secret of that strength ? If it can be shown that it was due to something inherent in Elijah, and peculiar to himself; some force of nature; some special quality of soul, to which ordinary men can lay no claim— then we may as well close our enquiries, and turn away from the inaccessible heights that mock us. But if it can be shown, as I think it can, that this splendid life was lived, not by its inherent qualities, but by sources of strength which are within the reach of the humblest child of God who reads these lines, then every line of it is an inspiration, beckoning us to its own glorious level. Courage, brothers ! There is nothing in this man's life which may not have its counterpart in ours, if only it can be established that his strength was obtained from sources which are accessible to ourselves.

Elijah's strength did not lie in himself or his surroundings. He was of humble extraction. He had no special training. He is expressly said to have been "a man of like passions" with ourselves. When, through failure of faith, he was cut off from the source of his strength, he showed more craven-hearted cowardice than most men would have done; he lay down upon the desert sands, asking to die. When the natural soil of his nature shows itself, it is not richer than that of the majority of men; and, if anything, it is the reverse.

ELIJAH GIVES US THREE INDICATIONS OF THE SOURCE OF HIS STRENGTH.

(1) "*As Jehovah liveth.*" To all beside, Jehovah might seem dead; but to him, He was the one supreme reality of life. And if we would be strong, we too must be able to say: "I know that my Redeemer liveth; He ever liveth to make intercession for us; and because He lives, we shall live also." The death of the Cross was bitter, but He liveth; the spear made fearful havoc, but He liveth; the grave was fast closed, but He liveth; men and devils did their worst, but He liveth. The man who has heard Jesus say, "I am He that liveth," will also hear him say, "Fear not! be strong, yea, be strong."

(2) "*Before whom I stand.*" He was standing in the presence of Ahab; but he was conscious of the presence of a greater than any earthly monarch, even the presence of Jehovah, before whom angels bow in lowly worship, hearkening to the voice of His word. Gabriel himself could not employ a loftier designation (Luke i. 19). Let us cultivate this habitual recognition of the presence of God; it will lift us above all other fear. Let us build our cottage so that every window may look out on the mighty Alps of God's presence; and that we may live, and move, and have our being, beneath the constant impression: "Lo, God is here." Besides this, a conviction had been borne in upon his mind that he was chosen by God, as His called and recognized servant and messenger; and in this capacity he stood before Him.

(3) The word "Elijah" may be rendered—Jehovah is my God; but there is another possible translation—JEHOVAH IS MY STRENGTH. This gives the key to his life. God was

the strength of his life; of whom should he be afraid?
When the wicked, even his enemies and foes, came on
him to eat up his flesh, they stumbled and fell. Though an
host should encamp against him, his heart should not fear.
What a revelation is given us in this name! Oh that it were
true of each of us! Yet, why should it not be? Let us from
henceforth cease from our own strength, which, at the best,
is weakness; and let us appropriate God's by daily, hourly
faith. Then this shall be the motto of our future lives:
"In the Lord have I righteousness and strength; I can do all
things through Christ which strengthened me; the Lord is
my strength and song, and He is become my salvation."

II

BESIDE THE DRYING BROOK
(1 KINGS XVII)

WE are studying the life of a man of like passions with ourselves—weak where we are weak, failing where we would fail; but who stood singlehanded against his people, and stemmed the tide of idolatry and sin, and turned a nation back to God. And he did it by the use of resources which are within reach of us all. This is the fascination of the story. Prove to us that he acted by the spell of some secret which is hidden from us meaner men; convince us that he was cast in an heroic mould to which we can lay no claim—then we must lay aside the story; disappointment has overcast our interest: it is a model we cannot copy; an ideal we cannot realize; a vision that mocks us as it fades into the azure of the past.

But this is not the case. This man, by whom God threshed the mountains, was only a worm at the best. This pillar in God's temple was, by nature, a reed shaken by the breath of the slightest zephyr. This Prophet of Fire, who shone like a torch, was originally but a piece of smoking flax. Faith made him all he became; and faith will do as much for us, if only we can exercise it as he did, to appropriate the might of the eternal God. All power is in God; and it hath pleased Him to store it all in the risen Saviour, as in some vast reservoir; and those stores are brought into human hearts by the Holy Ghost; and the Holy Ghost is given according to the measure of our receptivity and faith. Oh for Elijah's receptiveness, that we

19

might be as full of Divine power as he was; and as able, therefore, to do exploits for God and truth !

But, before this can happen, we must pass through the same education as he. You must go to Cherith and Zarephath before you can stand on Carmel. Even the faith you have must be pruned, and educated, and matured, that it may become strong enough to subdue kingdoms, work righteousness, and turn to flight armies of aliens.

Notice, then, the successive steps in God's education of His servants.

I. GOD'S SERVANTS MUST LEARN TO TAKE ONE STEP AT A TIME.

This is an elementary lesson; but it is hard to learn. No doubt Elijah found it so. Before he left Thisbe for Samaria, to deliver the message that burdened his soul, he would naturally inquire, what he should do when he had delivered it. How would he be received ? What would be the outcome ? Whither should he go to escape the vengeance of Jezebel, who had not shrunk from slaying with the sword prophets less dauntless than himself ? If he had asked those questions of God, and waited for a reply before he left his highland home, he would never have gone at all. Our Father never treats His children so. He only shows us one step at a time—and that, the next; and He bids us take it in faith. If we look up into His face, and say: "But if I take this step, which is certain to involve me in difficulty, what shall I do next ?" the heavens will be dumb, save with the one repeated message, "Take it, and trust Me."

But directly God's servant took the step to which he was led, and delivered the message, then "the word of the Lord came to him, saying: Get thee hence, hide thyself by the brook Cherith." So it was afterwards; it was only when the brook had dried up, and the stream had dwindled to pools, and the pools to drops, and the drops had died away in the sand—only then did the word of the Lord come to him, saying, "Arise, get thee to Zarephath."

I like that phrase, "the word of the Lord came to him." He did not need to go to search for it; it *came* to him. And so it will come to you. It may come through the Word of God; or through a distinct impression made on your heart by the Holy Ghost; or through circumstances: but it will find you out, and tell you what you are to do. "Lord, what wilt Thou have me to do? And the Lord said unto him, Arise, and go into the city, and it shall be told thee what thou must do" (Acts ix. 6).

It may be that for long you have had upon your mind some strong impression of duty; but you have held back, because you could not see what the next step would be. Hesitate no longer! Step out upon what seems to be the impalpable mist: you will find a slab of adamant beneath your feet; and, every time you put your foot forward, you will find that God has prepared a stepping-stone, and the next, and the next; each as you come to it. The bread is by the day. The manna is every morning. The strength is according to the moment's need. God does not give all the directions at once, lest we should get confused; He tells us just as much as we can remember and do. Then we must look to Him for more; and so we learn, by easy stages, the sublime habits of obedience and trust.

II. God's servants must be taught the value of the hidden life.

"Get thee hence, and turn thee eastward, and hide thyself by the brook Cherith." The man who is to take a high place before his fellows, must take a low place before his God; and there is no better manner of bringing a man down, than by dropping him suddenly out of a sphere to which he was beginning to think himself essential, teaching him that he is not at all necessary to God's plan; and compelling him to consider in the sequestered vale of some Cherith how mixed are his motives, and how insignificant his strength.

So the Master dealt with His Apostles. When, on one occasion, they returned to Him, full of themselves, and flushed with success, He quietly said, "Come ye yourselves apart into a desert place." We are too strong, too full of self, for God to use us. We vainly imagine that we are something, and that God cannot dispense with us. How urgently we need that God should bury our self-life in the darkness of a Cherith or a tomb, so as to hide it, and keep it in the place of death. We must not be surprised, then, if sometimes our Father says: "There, child, thou hast had enough of this hurry, and publicity, and excitement; get thee hence, and hide thyself by the brook—hide thyself in the Cherith of the sick chamber; or in the Cherith of disappointed hopes; or in the Cherith of bereavement; or in some solitude from which the crowds have ebbed away." Happy is he, who can reply, "This Thy will is also mine; I flee unto Thee to hide me. Hide me in the secret of Thy tabernacle; and beneath the covert of Thy wings!"

Every saintly soul that would wield great power with men must win it in some hidden Cherith. A Carmel triumph always pre-supposes a Cherith; and a Cherith always leads to a Carmel. We cannot give out unless we have previously taken in. We cannot exorcise the devils which possess men, unless we have first entered into our closets and shut our doors, and spent hours of rapt intercourse with God. The acquisition of spiritual power is impossible, unless we can hide ourselves from men and from ourselves in some deep gorge, where we may absorb the power of the eternal God; as vegetation through long ages absorbed those qualities of sunshine, which it now gives back through burning coal.

Bishop Andrewes had his Cherith, in which he spent five hours every day in prayer and devotion. John Welsh had it—who thought the day ill-spent which did not witness eight or ten hours of closet communion. David Brainard had it in the woods of North America, which were the favourite scene of his devotions. Christmas Evans had it in his long and lonely journeys amid the hills of Wales. Fletcher of Madeley had it—who would often leave his class-room for his private chamber, and spend hours upon his knees with his students, pleading for the fulness of the Spirit till they could kneel no longer. Or—passing back to the blessed age from which we date the centuries—Patmos, the seclusion of the Roman prisons, the Arabian desert, the hills and vales of Palestine, are for ever memorable as the Cheriths of those who have made our modern world. Our Lord found His Cherith at Nazareth, and in the wilderness of Judæa; amid the olives of Bethany, and the solitudes of Gadara. Not one of us therefore can dispense with some Cherith, where the sounds of earthly toil and human voices are exchanged for the murmur of the waters of quietness which are fed from the throne; and where we may taste the sweets and imbibe the power of a life hidden with Christ, and in Christ by the power of the Holy Ghost. Sometimes a human spirit, intent on its quest, may even find its Cherith in a crowd; of such a one God is its all-sufficient abode, and the secret place of the Most High its most holy place.

III. GOD'S SERVANTS MUST LEARN TO TRUST GOD ABSOLUTELY.

We yield at first a timid obedience to a command which seems to involve manifest impossibilities; but when we find that God is even better than His word, our faith groweth exceedingly, and we advance to further feats of faith and service. This is how God trains His young eaglets to fly. At last nothing is impossible. This is the key to Elijah's experience.

How strange to be sent to a brook, which would of course be as subject to the drought as any other! How contrary to nature to suppose that ravens, which feed on carrion, would find such food as man could eat; or, having found it, would bring it regularly morning and evening! How unlikely, too, that he could remain secreted from the search of the bloodhounds of Jezebel anywhere within the limits of Israel! But God's command was clear and unmistakable. It left him no alternative but to obey. "So he went and did according to the word of the Lord."

One evening, as we may imagine, Elijah reached the narrow gorge, down which the brook bounded with musical babble toward the Jordan. On either side the giant cliffs towered up, enclosing a little patch of blue sky. The interlacing boughs of the trees made a natural canopy in the hottest noon. All along the streamlet's course the moss would make a carpet of richer hue and softer texture than could be found in the palaces of kings. And, yonder, came the young ravens—"the young ravens that lack and suffer hunger," bringing bread and flesh. What a lesson was this of God's power to provide for his child! In after days Elijah would often recur to it, as dating a new epoch in his life. "I can never doubt God again. I am thankful that He shut me off from all other supplies, and threw me back on Himself. I am sure that He will never fail me, whatsoever the circumstances of strait or trial through which He may call me to pass."

There is strong emphasis on the word *there*. "I have commanded the ravens to feed thee *there*." Elijah might have preferred many hiding-places to Cherith; but that was the only place to which the ravens would bring his supplies; and, as long as he was there, God was pledged to provide for him. Our supreme thought should be: "Am I where God wants me to be?" If so, God will work a direct miracle, sooner than suffer us to perish for lack. If the younger son chooses to go to the far country of his own accord, he may be in danger of dying of starvation among his swine; but if the Father send him there, he shall have enough and to spare. God sends no soldier to the warfare on his own charges. He does not expect us to attend to the duties of the field and the commissariat. The manna always accompanies the pillar of cloud. If we do His will on earth as in heaven, He will give us daily bread. "Seek ye first the kingdom of God and His righteousness, and all these things shall be added unto you."

We will not stay to argue the probability of this story being true. It is enough that it is written here. And the presence of the supernatural presents no difficulties to those who can say "Our Father," and who believe in the resurrection of our Lord Jesus. But if corroboration were needed, it could be multiplied an hundredfold from the experience of living people, who have had their needs supplied in ways quite as marvellous as the coming of ravens to the lonely prophet.

A little boy, having read this incident with his widowed mother one wintry night, as they sat in a fireless room, beside a bare table, asked her if he might set the door open for God's ravens to come in; he was so sure that they must be on their way. The burgomaster of that German town, passing by, was attracted by the sight of the open door, and entered, inquiring the cause. When he learnt the reason, he said, "I will be God's raven"; and relieved their need then and afterwards. Ah, reader, God has an infinite fertility of resource; and if thou art doing His work, where He would have thee, He will supply thy need, though the heavens fall. Only trust Him!

IV. GOD'S SERVANTS ARE OFTEN CALLED TO SIT BY DRYING BROOKS.

"It came to pass after a while (*margin*, at the end of days) that the brook dried up." Our wildest fancy can but inadequately realize the condition to which the Land of Promise was reduced by the first few months of drought. The mountain pastures were seared as by the passage of fire. The woodlands and copses were scorched and silent. The rivers and brooks shrank attenuated in their beds; receding continually; and becoming daily more shallow and still. There was no rain to revive vegetation, or replenish the supplies of water. The sun rose and set for months in a sky, the blue of which was unflecked by a single cloud. There was no dew, to sprinkle the parched, cracked earth with refreshing tears. And so Cherith began to sing less cheerily. Each day marked a visible diminution of its stream. Its voice grew fainter and fainter; till its bed became a course of stones, baking in the scorching heat. It dried up.

What did Elijah think? Did he think that God had forgotten him? Did he begin to make plans for himself? This would have been human; but we will hope that he waited quietly for God, quieting himself as a weaned child, as he sang, "My soul, wait thou only upon God; for my expectation is from Him."

Many of us have had to sit by drying brooks; perhaps some are sitting by them now—the drying brook of popularity, ebbing away as from John the Baptist. The drying brook of health, sinking under a creeping paralysis, or a slow consumption. The drying brook of money, slowly dwindling before the demands of sickness, bad debts, or other people's extravagance. The drying brook of friendship, which for long has been diminishing, and threatens soon to cease. Ah, it is hard to sit beside a drying brook—much harder than to face the prophets of Baal on Carmel.

Why does God let them dry? He wants to teach us not to trust in His gifts but in Himself. He wants to drain us of self, as He drained the apostles by ten days of waiting before Pentecost. He wants to loosen our roots ere He removes us to some other sphere of service and education. He wants to put in stronger contrast the river of throne-water that never dries. Let us learn these lessons, and turn from our failing Cheriths to our unfailing Saviour. All sufficiency resides in Him—unexhausted by the flight of the ages; undiminished by the thirst of myriads of saints, who drink yonder in the uplands, near its source, as we do in these lower lands of earth and time. "The river of God is full of water." "He that drinketh of this water shall thirst again: but he that drinketh of the water that I shall give him shall never thirst; but it shall be in him a well of water, springing up into everlasting life." "Drink abundantly, O beloved!"

III

ORDERED TO ZAREPHATH
(1 KINGS XVII)

A FRIEND of mine, spending a few days in the neighbourhood of our English lakes, came upon the most beautiful shrubs he had ever seen. Arrested by their extraordinary luxuriance, he inquired the cause; and learnt that it was due to a judicious system of transplanting, constantly pursued. Whatever may be the effect of such a process in nature, it is certainly true that our heavenly Father employs similar methods to secure the highest results in us. He is constantly transplanting us. And though these changes threaten at times to hinder all steady progress in the Divine life, yet, if they are rightly borne, they result in the most exquisite manifestations of Christian character and experience.

Another illustration of the same truth is given by the prophet Jeremiah, when he says, "Moab hath been at ease from his youth; and he hath settled on his lees; and hath not been emptied from vessel to vessel; neither hath he gone into captivity: therefore his taste remained in him, and his scent is not changed" (Jer. xlviii. 11). Grape juice, when first expressed from its ruddy chalice, is impure and thick; it is left in vessels for a time till fermentation has done its work, and a thick sediment, called lees, has been precipitated to the bottom. When this is done, the liquid is carefully drawn off into another vessel, so that all the precipitated sediment is left behind. This emptying process is repeated again and again, till the offensive odour that

28

came from the "*must*" has passed away, and the liquid
has become clear and beautiful. In the case of Moab,
there had been none of this unsettling process; "he had
not been emptied from vessel to vessel," and in consequence
the people had made no moral or spiritual progress; "his
taste remained in him, and his scent was not changed."
The quiet life is by no means the greatest life. Some charac-
ters can only reach the highest standard of spirituality by
the disturbings or displacings in the order of God's
providence.

Will not this cast light upon God's dealings with Elijah ?
Once he stood in the vessel, "Home"; then emptied into
the vessel "Jezreel"; then into the vessel, "Cherith";
and now into the fourth vessel, "Zarephath": and all
that he might not settle upon his lees, but might be urged
towards a goal of moral greatness, which otherwise he
had never reached; but which qualified him to take his
stand in after-days on the Transfiguration Mount, the
associate of Moses, the companion of Christ. Take heart,
ye who are compelled to be constantly on the move—
pitching the tent to-night, and summoned by the moving
cloud and the trumpet call to strike it to-morrow; all this
is under the direction of a wise and faithful love, which is
educating you for a glorious destiny. Believe only that
your circumstances are those most suited to develop your
character. They have been selected out of all possible
combinations of events and conditions, in order to effect
in you the highest finish of usefulness and beauty; they
would have been the ones selected by you, if all the wide
range of omniscient knowledge had been within your
reach.

And yet, when a human spirit is entirely taken up with
God, as Elijah was, these changes become comparatively
harmless and trifling—as a gnat-sting to a soldier in the

heat of battle. To one who lives ever in the presence of the unchanging God, and who can say, "Thus saith Jehovah, before whom I stand," the ever-varying conditions of our lot touch only the outer rim of life; whatever they take away, they cannot take away *that*; whatever they bring, they cannot give more than *that*. The consciousness of that Presence is the one all-mastering thought; the inspiration, the solace, the comfort, of every waking hour. And as we have seen a far-spread summer landscape through the haze of intense heat, so do all people and things and events show themselves through the all-enwrapping, all-encompassing presence of God. To fulfil His plans; to obey the least intimation of His will; to wait on His hand; to dwell in the absorbing vision of Himself; to be satisfied with the fulness of joy which fills His presence-chamber with sweetest perfume and with celestial music—this is the one passion of the happy spirit, to whom, as to Elijah, this grace is given. But such grace is for thee, through the Holy Ghost, if only thou wilt open to it all the capacities of thy heart and life. Why not seek it?

There are several lessons here.

I. FAITH AWAITS GOD'S PLANS.

"It came to pass, after awhile, that the brook dried up, because there had been no rain in the land." Week after week, with unfaltering and steadfast spirit, Elijah watched that dwindling brook; often tempted to stagger through unbelief, but refusing to allow his circumstances to come between himself and God. Unbelief sees God through circumstances, as we sometimes see the sun shorn of his rays through the smoky air; but faith puts God between itself and circumstances, and looks at them through Him. And so the dwindling brook became a silver thread; and the silver thread stood presently in pools at the foot of the largest boulders; and then the pools shrank. The birds fled; the wild creatures of field and forest came no more to drink; the brook was dry. Only then, to his patient and unwavering spirit "the word of the Lord came, saying, Arise, get thee to Zarephath."

Most of us would have got anxious and worn with planning long before that. We should have ceased our songs, as soon as the streamlet carolled less musically over its rocky bed; and with harps swinging on the willows we should have paced to and fro upon the withering grass, lost in pensive thought. And, probably, long ere the brook was dry, we should have devised some plan, and asking God's blessing on it, would have started off elsewhere. Alas! we are all too full of our own schemes, and plans, and contrivings. And if Samuel does not come just when we expect, we force ourselves, and offer the burnt-offering (1 Sam. xiii. 12). This is the source of untold misery. We sketch out our programme, and rush into it; and only when we are met by insuperable obstacles do we begin to reflect whether it was God's will, or to appeal to Him. He does often extricate us, because His mercy endureth for ever; but if we had only waited first to see the unfolding of His plans, we should never have found ourselves landed in such an inextricable labyrinth; and we should never have been compelled to retrace our steps with so many tears of shame.

One of the formative words for all human lives, and especially for God's servants, was given by God to Moses, when He said: "See that thou make all things according to the pattern showed to thee in the mount" (Heb. viii. 5). Moses was eager to do God's work, and the best skill amongst the people was at his command; but he must not make a single bell, or pomegranate, or tassel, or fringe, or curtain, or vessel, except on God's pattern, and after God's ideal. And so he was taken up into the mount, and God opened the door into his own mind, where the tabernacle stood complete as an ideal; and Moses was permitted to see the thing as it lived in the thought and heart of God. Forty days of reverent study passed by; and when he returned to the mountain-foot, he had only to transfer into the region of actual fact that which had been already shown to him, in pattern, on the Mount.

Surely some such thought as this must have been in the mind of our blessed Lord, when He said: "The Son can do nothing of Himself, but what He seeth the Father do" (John v. 19). So utterly had He emptied Himself, that He had abandoned even His own schemes and plans; He lived a planless life, accepting each moment the plan which His Father unfolded before Him; and being confident that that plan would lead Him on to greater and ever greater works, until the world should marvel at the splendour of the results—rising from Gethsemane and Calvary, through the broken grave, to the Ascension Mount, and the glory of His second Advent. Oh, mystery of humiliation, that He who planned all things should will to live a life of such absolute dependence! And yet, if He lived such a life, how much more will it become us; how much anxiety it will save us; and to what lengths of usefulness and heights of glory will it bring us! Would that we were content to wait for God to unveil His plan, so that our life might be simply the working out of His thought, the exemplification of His ideal! Let this be the cry of our hearts: "Lord, show me Thy way; teach me to do Thy will: show me the way wherein I should walk, for unto Thee do I lift up my soul."

11. GOD'S PLANS DEMAND IMPLICIT OBEDIENCE.

"So he arose and went to Zarephath," as before he had gone to Cherith, and as presently he would go to show himself to Ahab. A Christian lady, who had learnt amongst us the blessedness of a surrendered life, and was soon after obliged to find another home across the ocean, came back quite recently, over thousands of miles of land and water, to visit the scene of that act, in the hope that she would find again her former joy, which had faded like the hues of a too radiant dawn. But to her disappointment, though she worshipped on the same sacred spot, and listened to the sounds of the well-known voice, she could not recover the priceless jewel she had lost. At last the cause appeared. She had been living in conscious disobedience to the will of Christ, expressed through her conscience and His Word. The motives that prompted the disobedience had a touch of nobility about them; but it was disobedience still, and it wrought its own penalty.

This is the true cause of failure in so many Christian lives. We catch sight of God's ideal; we are enamoured with it; we vow to be only His; we use the most emphatic words; we dedicate ourselves upon the altar. For awhile we seem to tread another world, bathed in heavenly light. Then there comes a command clear and unmistakable. We must leave some beloved Cherith, and go to some unwelcome Zarephath; we must speak some word, take some step, cut off some habit: and we shrink from it—the cost is too great. But, directly we refuse obedience, the light dies off the landscape of our lives, and dark clouds fling their shadows far and near.

We do not win salvation by our obedience; that is altogether the gift of God, to be received by faith in the finished work of Jesus Christ our Lord. But, being saved,

we must obey. Our Saviour adjures us, by the love we bear
to Himself, to keep His commandments. And He does so
because he wants us to taste His rarest gifts; and because
He knows that in the keeping of His commandments
there is great reward.

Search the Bible from board to board, and see if strict,
implicit, and instant obedience has not been the secret of
the noblest lives that ever lit up the dull monotony of the
world. The proudest title of our King was the Servant of
Jehovah. And none of us can seek to realize a nobler aim
than that which was the inspiration of His heart: "I come
to do Thy will, O my God." Mary, the simple-hearted
mother, uttered a word which is pertinent to every age,
when, at the marriage-feast, she turned to the servants and
said, "Whatsoever He saith unto you, do it."

III. IMPLICIT OBEDIENCE SOMETIMES BRINGS US INTO A
SMELTING-FURNACE.

"Zarephath" means a smelting-furnace. It lay outside
the Land of Canaan, occupying the site of the modern
Surafend, which stands on a long ridge, backed by the
snow-clad steeps of Hermon, and overlooking the blue
waters of the Mediterranean. Many things might have made
it distasteful to the prophet. It belonged to the land from
which Jezebel had brought her impious tribe. It was as
much cursed by the terrible drought as Canaan. It was
impossible to reach it save by a weary journey of 100 miles
through the heart of the land, where his name was execrated,
and his person proscribed. And then to be sustained by a
widow woman belonging to a heathen people ! He would
not have so much minded to have sustained her; but it was
not pleasant to feel that he must be dependent on her
slender earnings or meagre store. Surely it was a smelting-

furnace for cleansing out any alloy of pride, or self-reliance, or independence which might be lurking in the recesses of his heart.

And there was much of the refining fire in the character of his reception. When he reached the straggling town it was probably toward nightfall; and at the city gate a widow woman was gathering a few sticks to prepare the evening meal. To some it might have seemed a coincidence; but there is no such word in faith's vocabulary—that which to human judgment is a coincidence, to faith is a Providence. This was evidently the widow of whom God had spoken. Faint with thirst, and weary with long travel, but never doubting that his needs would be amply met, he asked her to fetch a little water in a vessel, that he might drink. The widow may have had some premonition of his coming. There would seem to be some suggestion of this having been so, in the words, "*I have commanded* a widow woman to sustain thee." Her character will come out in due course; but there must have been something in her which could not be found in the many widows of the land of Israel (Luke iv. 25, 26). It was for no arbitrary reason that God passed them over, and went so far afield. She must have possessed qualities of character, germs of better things, sparks of heroism and of faith, which distinguished her from all her sorrowing sisterhood, and made her the befitting hostess of the prophet, and the glad sharer with him in his Father's bounty. To her the impression was probably given of the coming of the prophet--just as the visions to Saul and to Ananias, to Cornelius and to Peter, flashed upon them in duplicates.

She was not, therefore, surprised at the prophet's request, and silently went to fetch a cup of cold water (Matt. x. 42). Encouraged by her willingness, Elijah asked her to bring with her a morsel of bread. It was a modest request;

but it unlocked the silent agony of her soul. She had not a cake, but a handful of meal in a barrel, and a little oil in a cruse; and she was about to make one last repast for herself and her son, who was probably too weak through long privation to be with her; and, having eaten it, they had no alternative but to lie down together and die. It was very depressing for the man of God, after his long and weary march.

It is thus that God leads His people still. "All that abideth not the fire, ye shall make go through the water," *i.e.*, He will not suffer us to be tempted beyond that which we are able to bear; He will not thresh vetches with a sharp threshing instrument, nor turn a cartwheel about on cummin. But it is written, "Everything that may abide the fire, ye shall make it go through the fire, and it shall be clean" (Num. xxxi. 23). If, then, there is aught in you that can bear the ordeal, be sure you will be put into the furnace. But the fire shall not destroy; it shall only cleanse you. You will be put into it by the hand of Love; and kept in it only till patience has done her perfect work. The flames shall only consume the bonds that bind you; and, as you walk loose in the fire, bystanders shall descry at your side the form of one like unto the Son of God.

IV. When God puts His people into the furnace, He will supply all their need.

Circumstances were certainly very depressing; but what are they to a man whose inner self is occupied with the presence and power of God? God had said that he should be fed, and by that widow; and so it should be, though the earth and heaven should pass away. Difficulties are to faith what gymnastic apparatus are to boys, means of

strengthening the muscular fibre. Like the fabled sala-
mander, faith feeds on fire. And so with heroic faith
Elijah said: "Fear not; go and do as thou hast said: for
thus saith the Lord God of Israel, The barrel of meal shall
not waste, neither shall the cruse of oil fail, until the day
that the Lord sendeth rain upon the earth."

Our only need is to inquire if we are at that point in
God's pattern where He would have us be. If we are,
though it seem impossible for us to be maintained, the
thing impossible shall be done. We shall be sustained by
a miracle, if no ordinary means will suffice. "Seek ye first
the kingdom of God and His righteousness, and all
these things shall be added unto you." We reserve for
future thought that unfailing meal and oil. But, ere we
close, remark with what different meaning different
people may use the same holy words. The widow said,
as Elijah had done, "The Lord God liveth" (1 Kings xvii.
12). But to her those words brought no comfort; because
they were repeated from hearsay, and not from a living
experience of their truth. God forbid that they should be a
parrot-speech upon your lips, my reader! but, rather,
may they be burnt into your inmost being—so that you
may go through life fearless of all save sin; and cheering
timid hearts with the assurance of an unfaltering courage,
"Fear not!" (ver. 13).

IV

"THE SPIRIT AND POWER OF ELIAS"
(1 KINGS XVII)

WHO that have travelled in Switzerland can forget the early mornings, when they have been summoned from sleep to await the dawn? A weird and mysterious hush possesses nature—as a crowd is hushed in expectancy of a king's approach. Then a strange light spreads outward from the eastern sky; at last one of the loftiest Alps is smitten with the roseate flush of dawn; then another, and another, and yet another, till the whole sisterhood of peaks, mantled with untrodden snow, is lit up and transfigured with burning splendour. But during all this time, the valleys below are swathed in mist, and veiled in darkness. And it is only after hours have passed away, and the monarch of the day has climbed slowly towards his throne, that the blessed sunlight penetrates to the tiny hamlets and scattered châlets, or sparkles in the brooks, or casts shadows from the stones and flowers.

This illustration will serve to show the difference between the dispensation which closed with the first advent of our Lord, and that in which it is our happiness to live, and which is to close with His glorious Epiphany. Each has been blessed with the ministry of the Holy Ghost; but it is in this age alone, dating from the Day of Pentecost, that He has been poured forth, on sons and daughters, on servants and handmaidens (Acts ii. 17). In the previous age He was bestowed, in His especial grace and fulness, only on the *élite* of the household of faith. Now every lowland

38

valley, the humblest and the weakest, may be bathed in His Divine and sacred influence; but in Elijah's time, those only who were Alpine in the elevation of their character knew what His eternal fulness meant. "Holy men of God spake as they were moved by the Holy Ghost." "The prophets searched what the Spirit of Christ which was in them did signify." "The Holy Ghost was not yet given, because that Jesus was not yet glorified."

Elijah was one of these men filled with the Holy Ghost. This was the universal testimony of those who knew him best. Elisha's one desire was that he should be heir to the Spirit which was so manifestly upon his master (2 Kings ii. 9). "The spirit of Elijah" was a familiar phrase on the lips of the sons of the prophets (2 Kings ii. 15). And years after, when the angel of God spake to Zacharias in the Temple, he could find no better illustration of the presence of the Holy Ghost in his promised child, than by saying, "He shall go before Him in the spirit and power of Elias" (Luke i. 15–17).

The glorious ministry of Elijah was therefore due, not to any inherent qualities in himself, but to the extraordinary indwelling of the Holy Ghost—given to him as to other holy men of God, in the old time—through faith. If then we could but have that same Spirit in an equal measure, we should be able to repeat his marvellous deeds. It is said that it would be possible to gather up the mighty force of Niagara, and, transforming it into electricity, carry it along a wire to drive machinery one hundred miles away: if this should ever be done, it would be a matter of almost perfect indifference whether the wire were slender or thick; the mighty force could as well travel along the slender thread, and as well perform its marvels, as through an electric cable. So the question for us all is, whether the Holy Ghost is working with and through us in power; if

He be, then, though our nature be paltry and weak, He shall effect through us the same mighty deeds as through men vastly our superiors in mental and moral force. Nay, we may even glory in our infirmities, that this Divine power may rest upon us more conspicuously, and that the glory may be more evidently God's.

Now the question arises: May we, ordinary Christian people, living in this nineteenth century, hope to receive the Holy Spirit in that extraordinary and especial measure in which He rested upon Elijah? Of course we have all received the Holy Spirit to a certain extent, or we could never have come to Jesus. All the graces of the Christian character, all our comfort, all our overcomings, are due to His presence.

> "*And every virtue we possess,*
> *And every victory won,*
> *And every thought of holiness,*
> *Are His alone.*"

And yet it is clear that over and beyond this ordinary grace, which all believers must have, there is a blessed anointing of the Holy Ghost which gives special equipment and fitness for service. Elijah had it. Our blessed Lord, as the perfect servant, had it; when, being full of the Holy Ghost, He returned in the power of the Spirit into Galilee, and traced His marvellous power to the fact of the Holy Spirit being upon Him (Luke iv. 1, 14, 18). The Apostles had it from the Day of Pentecost, when they received the fulness of the Spirit for witness-bearing; although they must have possessed Him before for personal character (compare Acts i. 8 and ii. 4 with John xx. 22). The Samaritan believers had it; but only after Peter and John had prayed for them, "that they might receive the Holy

Ghost"—although it is evident that their previous conversion and joy had been due to His blessed work (Acts viii. 15, 16). The disciples at Ephesus had it; but only after Paul had laid his hands upon them.

This is surely what we want. And this is what we may have. This special anointing for service is not only for men like Elijah, or Paul, or Peter, who soar far beyond us into the azure skies; but for us all, so long as there stands upon the page of revelation these priceless words, "The promise (referring obviously to Acts i. 4) is unto you, and to your children, and to all that are afar off, even as many as the Lord our God shall call" (Acts ii. 39). We are amongst the *far-off* ones; and therefore we may claim the promise for ourselves, and receive the fulness of the Holy Ghost, to equip us for our life and ministry.

But there are three conditions with which we must comply, if we would receive and keep this blessed gift.

I. WE MUST BE EMPTIED.

God cannot fill us if we are already filled. It took ten days to drain the Apostles, even though they had spent three years under the immediate tuition of Christ; but the emptying process was an indispensable preliminary to the Day of Pentecost. For Elijah, this process went on beside the drying brook, and during the long and dreary march to Zarephath, and throughout his sojourn there. It took apparently three years and six months. It was a long and weary waiting time, but it was well spent; for in proportion as he became emptied of self, and self-sufficiency, and self-dependence, he became filled with the Spirit of Power: so that Carmel itself, with all its heroic deeds, was gloriously possible to him.

Are we willing to pay this price ? Are we prepared for God to empty us of all that is in any wise contrary to His will ? Are we content to be empty and broken vessels, that the river, in whose bed we lie, may easily flow through us ? If not, let us ask Him to work in us to will His own good pleasure—plunging the cold stubborn iron into the glowing furnace of His grace; till it can be bent into perfect conformity to His own glorious will. But if we are willing, let us present our emptied nature to the Son of God, that He may fill us with the fulness of the Spirit. Let us also believe that He does fill us, so soon as we yield ourselves to Him. You do not want more of Him more urgently than He wants more of you; and the one is the condition of the other (Jas. iv. 5, R.V.). Grace, like nature, abhors a vacuum; and just as the cold fresh air will rush in to fill an exhausted receiver, as soon as it has a chance to enter, so does the grace of the Holy Spirit enter the heart that can boast of nothing but an aching void. There may be no ecstasy, no rushing wind, no fiery baptism; but, nevertheless, " the Lord, whom ye seek, shall suddenly come to His Temple," in floods of silent and golden light. " Thus saith the Lord, Make this valley full of ditches: for thus saith the Lord, Ye shall not see wind, neither shall ye see rain; yet that valley shall be filled with water " (2 Kings iii. 16, 17).

Many Christians, seeking this blessed fulness, make the same mistake as is so constantly made by seekers after forgiveness and acceptance with God. They look within for evidences of the reception and indwelling of the Spirit, and refuse to believe in His presence unless they detect certain symptoms and signs which they consider befitting. This is entirely wrong. The reckoning is not of feeling, but of faith.

If we have complied with God's directions, we must

believe, whether we feel any difference or not, that God has done His part, and has kept His promise, given us through Jesus Christ our Lord; and that He has not been slower to give the Holy Spirit than earthly fathers to give bread to their hungry children (Luke xi. 13). When we leave the chamber where we have solemnly dedicated ourselves to God, and sought to be filled with the Spirit, we must not examine our feelings to discover whether there is such a difference in us as we might expect; but we must cry, in the assurance of faith: " I praise Thee, Blessed One, that Thou hast not failed to perform Thy chosen work; Thou hast entered my longing heart; Thou hast taken up Thine abode in me: henceforth Thou shalt have Thy way with me, to will and do Thine own good pleasure."

We should not seek to know the presence of the Holy Ghost by any signs pointing to Himself. He reveals not Himself, but Christ. He glorifies Him (John xvi. 14). And the surest symptoms that He is within are—sensitiveness as to sin, tenderness of conscience, and the growing preciousness of Jesus, the fragrance of His name, sympathy with his purposes. Hast thou these in growing measure? Then dost thou know somewhat of His gracious filling.

A little child was once asked her age; and she replied, " I don't feel like seven. I feel like six; but mother says I'm seven." Here was the reckoning of faith, putting her mother's word before her own feeling. And thus we must refuse to consider ourselves, to diagnose our symptoms, or feel our pulse; but must launch out upon the deep of God's truthfulness, and let down our nets for a draught of power and blessing.

II. We must be obedient.

We have already insisted on this; but it is so indispensable, that repeated emphasis must be laid upon it. Christ reiterated His appeals for the keeping of His commands, in almost every sentence of His closing discourses with His disciples (John xiv. 15, 21, 23, 24). He gives the secret of His own abiding in His Father's love in these striking words: " As the Father gave Me commandment, even so I do. If ye keep My commandments, ye shall abide in My love; even as I have kept My Father's commandments, and abide in His love " (John xv. 10). Instant and implicit obedience to the teaching of the Word, and to the inner promptings of the Holy Spirit, is an absolute condition of keeping, or increasing, the store of sacred influence. On the contrary, one little item of disobedience persisted in is quite sufficient to check all further bestowments, and even to deprive us of what we have. " If ye be willing and obedient, ye shall eat the good of the land; but if ye refuse and rebel, ye shall be devoured with the sword." Nor is such obedience hard; for all God's commands are enablings, and His grace is sufficient. Look out for it. If only every believer who reads these lines would resolve from this hour to imitate Elijah, who went and did according to the word of the Lord (1 Kings xvii. 5 and 10)—not with the thought of merit, but beneath the inspiration of love; not in the weightier matters only, but in the crossings of the *t's*, and in the dottings of the *i's*—they would find at once that there would open before them a life of almost inconceivable glory. It is from the heights of unwavering obedience that we catch sight of the wide and open sea of blessedness. The exact obedience of Elias is the inviolable condition of receiving and keeping " the Spirit and Power of Elias."

III. WE MUST LIVE ON THE WORD OF GOD.

Elijah, the widow, and her son, lived on their daily replenished stores; but the prophet had other meat to eat which they knew not of: " Man shall not live by bread alone, but by every word that proceedeth out of the mouth of God." It was on that word that Elijah fed during those long and slow-moving days. Sometimes he would climb the heights behind the little town, in deep meditation upon that Word which is like the great mountains; and sometimes he would pace the sea-strand, musing on those judgments which are a great deep. He could say with another: " Thy words were found, and I did eat them; and Thy Word was unto me the joy and rejoicing of my heart." And sitting with the widow and her son, he would make that Word the topic of his constant talk; so that she was compelled to refer to it in these significant terms: " I know that the word of the Lord in thy mouth is truth " (1 Kings xvii. 24).

The importance of feeding on the Word of God is affirmed by our Lord, when He says: " As the living Father hath sent Me, and I live by the Father; so he that eateth Me, even he shall live by Me." We eat our Lord's flesh when we meditate lovingly upon His Word. The Word is in the words. His words are spirit and life.

This is the further absolute condition of becoming and remaining filled with the Holy Ghost. The Spirit works with and through the Word. What the metal is to the locomotive; what the wire is to the electric spark; what the grammar is to the teacher; what the corn-grain is to the spirit of life—that the Word of God is to the Spirit of God. If then we neglect the reverent study of Scripture, we cut ourselves off from the very vehicle through which God's Spirit enters human spirits. And this is the great fault of our times. Christian people will attend conventions, plunge into all kinds of Christian work, read many good books about the Bible and Christian living; but they give the Bible itself the most cursory and superficial heed. And it is for this reason that the Bible does not speak to them.

If you would know all the wondrous beauty of a forest glade, you must not be satisfied with passing through it with hasty foot, and in company with a troop of merry children, whose ringing laughter carries panic into the hearts of thousands of shy living things that, with trembling hearts, keep still in hole, and brake, and nest. No; you must go alone, and sit quietly down on the log of some felled tree, and wait. Then the mystery of beauty will begin to unfold itself: the fairy bowers, the mossy glens, the interlacing boughs. Presently a note will sound from yonder bough, as the signal for the outburst of many sweet-voiced choristers, and the woodland will ring with the music of the birds; whilst the squirrel runs up some neighbouring tree, and the rabbits come out to feed, and the young foxes play about their holes. All this is hidden from those who cannot wait. So there are mysteries of glory and beauty in Scripture hidden from the wise and prudent, but revealed to babes. There is no book that will so repay time spent over its pages as the Word of God.

A neglected Bible means a starved and strengthless spirit; a comfortless heart; a barren life; and a grieved Holy Ghost. If the people, who are now perpetually running about to meetings for crumbs of help and comfort, would only stay at home and search their Bibles, there would be more happiness in the Church, and more blessing on the world. It is very prosaic counsel; but it is true.

We must reserve for our next chapter some account of the life which this Spirit-filled man lived in the little household with which he dwelt. Suffice it now to say that the

Holy Ghost, which dwelt in him so largely, revealed Himself in those very traits which must always be His fruits: gentleness under provocation; steadfastness in trial; power in prayer; life victorious over death. But we may note, in closing, the remarkable admission of the widow: " I know that thou art a man of God " (1 Kings xvii. 24).

We talk of the man of letters, the man of honour, the man of mark; but how infinitely better to be known as a man of God—one of God's men, a man after God's own heart! And how splendid the tribute, when we are so addressed by those with whom we have been wont to live! That "familiarity breeds contempt" is one of the world's common-places; but when a man is filled with the Holy Ghost, the more he is known, the more clearly he is proved to be a man of God.

And the power of the indwelling Spirit evinced itself, in Elijah's case, in the marvellous effect produced on that widow and her child. The widow was convinced of sin, and led to the truth of God. The son was brought back from death into a resurrection-life. And such results shall accrue in your experience, if you will only seek to be filled with the fulness of God. " He that believeth in Me, the works that I do shall he do also; and greater works than these shall he do; because I go unto my Father." " Ye shall receive power, after that the Holy Ghost is come upon you."

V

The Test of the Home-Life
(1 Kings xvii)

MANY a man might bear himself as a hero and saint in the solitudes of Cherith, or on the heights of Carmel, and yet wretchedly fail in the home-life of Zarephath. It is one thing to commune with God in the solitudes of nature, and to perform splendid acts of devotion and zeal for Him in the presence of thousands; but it is quite another to walk with Him day by day in the midst of a home, with its many calls for the constant forgetfulness of self. Blessed, indeed, is the home-life on whose threshold we cast aside our reserve, our attitude of self-defence, our suspicions and our fears; and resign ourselves to the unquestioning trust of those whose love puts the tenderest construction on much that the world exaggerates and distorts!

And yet it would be idle to deny that there is much to try and test us just where the flowers bloom, and the voices of hate and passion die away in distant murmurs. There is a constant need for the exercise of gentleness, patience, self-sacrifice, self-restraint. And beneath the test of home, with its incessant duties and demands, many men break down, whose character seems, like some Alpine peak, to shoot up far beyond the average of those with whom they associate in the busy world.

This ought not so to be; nor need it be. If our religion is what it should be, it will resemble the law of gravitation; which not only controls the planets in their spheres, but guides the course of each dust-grain through the autumn

breeze, and determines the fall of a rose-leaf fluttering to
the path. Everything will come beneath its sway—each
look, each word, each trivial act. Indeed we shall show the
reality and thoroughness of our religion, when it is no
longer a garment, to be put off and on at will; but when it
pervades us, as life does the organism in which it is contained. The truly religious man will be as sweet in irritating
gnat-stings as in crushing calamities; as self-denying for a
child as for a crowd; as patient over a spoilt or late meal as
over an operation which summons all his manhood to the
front. " My grace is sufficient for thee," is the one answer
of Jesus Christ to all inquiries; the one reply to all excuses
and complaints about trying circumstances.

Thy home-life was chosen for thee by the unerring skill
of One who knows thee better than thou knowest thyself,
and who could not mistake. It has been selected as the
best school of grace for thee. Its burdens were poised on
the hand of infinite love, before they were placed on thy
shoulders. Its pressure has been carefully measured by
scales more delicate than those which chemists use. And
now, looking down upon thee, the Master says: " There is
nothing in thy life that may not be lived in Me, for Me,
through Me: and I am willing to enable thee to be sweet
and noble and saint-like in it all."

In our last chapter, we saw something of the power and
Spirit with which Elijah was filled and endued. It was
nothing less than the Holy Ghost Himself; and we learnt
that that same glorious gift is for each of us. Indeed, it is
our bounden duty never to rest until we are filled with that
same fullness, and clothed in that same robe. But we are
now to follow him into a home, and see how he bears the
test of home life; and we shall learn to admire and love
him the more. He lived a truly human life; he was not

*" Too great or good
For human nature's daily food."*

He was the same man in the widow's house as on
Carmel's heights. He is like one of those mountains to
which we have referred, piercing the heavens with unscale-
able heights; but clothed about the lower parts with woodlands, and verdant fields, and smiling bowers, where bees
gather honey, and children play. He shows that when a
man is full of the Holy Ghost, it will be evidenced by the
entire tenour of his daily walk and conversation. In this
he reminds us of Luther, the Elijah of modern times, who
stood alone against the apostasy of the Romish church;
but whose family life was a model of beauty—an oasis in
the desert. Let those, who only know him as the Reformer,
read his letters to his little daughter; and they will be
captivated by the winsomeness and tenderness of that great
and gentle soul.

I. ELIJAH TEACHES US CONTENTMENT.

The fare in the widow's home was frugal enough; and
there was only just sufficient of it for their daily needs.
Human nature, which was as strong in the prophet as in
the rest of us, would have preferred to be able to count
sacks of meal and barrels of oil. It would have been
pleasant to go into some spacious storeroom, and, looking
around on the abundant provision, to say: " Soul, thou
hast goods enough to carry thee through the years of
famine: take thine ease, eat, drink, and be merry." But
this is not God's way; nor is it the healthiest discipline for
our better life.

God's rule is—day by day. The manna fell on the
desert sands day by day. Our bread is promised to us for
the day. As our day, so will our strength be. And they

who live like this are constantly reminded of their blessed dependence on their Father's love; they are led back again to the life of the little child; they know nothing of those temptations to self-sufficiency which work ruin to the rich—as the growth of the southern seas silently eats away the bottoms of the mighty vessels which defy the storms, but become the prey of myriads of minute insects, working always out of sight.

If God were to give us the choice between seeing our provision and keeping it ourselves, or not seeing it and leaving Him to deal it out, day by day, most of us would be almost sure to choose the former alternative. It gratifies our sense of importance to count up our stores, our barrels, and our sacks; it invests us with so much superiority to our neighbours; it gives such a sense of security. But we should be far wiser to say, " I am content to trust Thee, Father, the living God, who givest us all things richly to enjoy. Keep Thou the stores under Thine own hand, they will give me less anxiety; they will not lead me into temptation; they will not expose me to be jealous of others less favoured than myself."

And those who live thus are not worse off than others. Nay, in the truest sense, they are better off. Better off, because the responsibility of maintaining them rests wholly upon God; and they are delivered from the fret of anxiety, the strain of daily care, and the temptations which make it almost impossible for a rich man to enter the Kingdom of God. If God guarantees, as He does, our support, does it much matter whether we can *see* the sources from which He will obtain it ? It might gratify our curiosity, but it would not make them more sure. They are as really in existence, and beneath His eye; and they will as really come safely to our hand. The main thing is to understand the precious promise, " Seek ye first the kingdom of God and His righteousness, and all these things shall be added unto you." Then let us go on doing our duty, filling our time, working out the plan of our life. We may be as free from care as the birds, that have neither storehouse nor barn. We may laugh as merrily as the child, who comes in from school to eat, and goes out again to play, and is utterly thoughtless about its next meal. We may be entirely destitute, our pantry bare, our money exhausted, our means of livelihood gone. But our Father has ample resources: His are the cattle on a thousand hills; and His the waving corn-fields, and the myriad fish of the ocean depths; His hired servants have bread enough and to spare; He has prepared a supply for our need, and He will deliver it to time, if only we will trust Him.

It is impossible to tell whose eyes may read these words; but if they should be read by those whose one aim it is to be *independent*, let them consider what they mean. Do they mean to be independent of God, or of men? In point of fact, they will live to see that they can be independent of neither. And the serious question presents itself, Is this a worthy aim for those who are the bought slaves of Christ? Surely we are meant to be stewards; not storing up our Lord's money for ourselves, but administering for Him all that we do not need for the maintenance of ourselves and our dear ones, in the position of life in which God has placed us. And our only worldly aim should be to lay out our Lord's money to the very best advantage; so that we may render Him an account with joy, when He comes to reckon with us.

If, on the other hand, these words are read by those who are dependent on daily supplies—with little hope of ever owning more than the daily handful of meal, and the little oil at the bottom of the cruse—let them be comforted by the example of Elijah. " Be content with such things as ye have; for He hath said, I will never leave thee, nor forsake thee " (Heb. xiii. 5). The bottom of the barrel may have been scraped to-day; but on going to it to-morrow there will be just enough for to-morrow's needs. The last drop of oil may have been drained to-day; but there will be more to-morrow, and enough. Anxiety will not do you good; but the prayer of faith will. " Your Father knoweth what things ye have need of." He who lit life's flame knows how much fuel is required to keep it burning. Throw all responsibility on God. He who gave His own Son will with Him freely give all things. Do not listen to the arch-liar, who bids you distrust and despair: he has never yet been justified by the event; his prophecies have always proved false; his insinuations are simply beds of rank and poisonous stinging-nettles—do not lie down in them, but trample them beneath your feet. Oh that we might learn, though it be in the school of privation, in whatsoever state we are, therewith to be content; and to be able to cry, with one of Elijah's compeers, " I can do all things through Christ, which strengtheneth me." " For thus saith the Lord God of Israel: The barrel of meal shall not waste, neither shall the cruse of oil fail, until the day that the Lord sendeth rain upon the earth."

II. ELIJAH ALSO TEACHES US GENTLENESS UNDER PROVOCATION.

We do not know how long the mother hung over her dying child. He may have been struck down like the little fellow who cried, " My head ! my head ! " and faded in one summer's afternoon; or he may have lingered beneath the spell of a wearying illness, which not only wore out his life, but overtaxed his mother's nerves so that she spoke unadvisedly and cruelly to the man who had brought deliverance to her home: " Art thou come to call my sin to remembrance, and to slay my son ? "

A remark, so uncalled-for and unjust, might well have stung the prophet to the quick, or prompted a bitter reply. And it would have doubtless done so, had his goodness been anything less than inspired by the Holy Ghost. But one of the fruits of His indwelling is Gentleness. " The fruit of the Spirit is love, joy, peace, long-suffering, *gentleness*." The nature breathed into the spirit by the blessed Spirit of God is identical with His own, which is Love: and " Love suffereth long and is kind; is not easily provoked; beareth all things; believeth all things; hopeth all things; endureth all things." Thus it happened, that without further remark Elijah simply said, " Give me thy son." If there were a momentary uprising of indignation, it was immediately quelled by the Dove which had come to brood in the nest of his heart.

We need more of this practical godliness. Many deceive themselves. They go to fervid meetings, and profess that they have placed all upon the altar; they speak as if they were indeed filled with the Holy Ghost. But when they return to their homes, the least friction, or interference with their plans, or mistake on the part of others, or angry outburst, arouses a sudden and violent manifestation of temper. Such people have not yet experienced His special grace; there is much more for them to learn. He who first led them to Jesus is able to make them meek with His meekness, and gentle with His gentleness; He can give them victory over their natural infirmities, as well as over all conscious sin; He can work so great a transformation within them, that " instead of the thorn shall come up the fir tree, and instead of the brier shall come up the myrtle tree; and it shall be to the Lord for a name, for an everlasting sign that shall not be cut off."

If the Holy Spirit is really filling the heart, there will come over the rudest, the least refined, the most selfish, a marvellous change; there will be a gentleness in speech, in the very tones of the voice; a tender thoughtfulness in the smallest actions; a peace passing understanding on the face; and these shall be the evident seal of the Holy Ghost, the mint-mark of heaven. Are they evident in ourselves ?

> " Gentle Spirit, dwell with me,
> I myself would gentle be;
> And with words that help and heal,
> Would Thy life in mine reveal."

III. ELIJAH TEACHES ALSO THE POWER OF A HOLY LIFE.

Somewhere in the background of this woman's life there was a dark deed, which dwarfed all other memories of wrong-doing, and stood out before her mind as her sin— " my sin " (1 Kings xvii. 18). What it was we do not know; it may have been connnected with the birth of that very son. It had probably been committed long years before, and had then filled her with a keen agony of mind; for conscience is not inoperative even in the hearts of the children of idolatry and heathendom (Rom. ii. 14, 15). But of later years, the keen sense of remorse had become dulled; conscience long outraged had grown benumbed; sometimes she even lost all recollection of her sin for weeks and months together. We all have a wonderful faculty of dismissing from us an unwelcome thought; just as men try to hide from themselves the too-evident symptoms of a disease which is sapping the forces of life.

There is a wonderful invention, recently perfected, by which sound can be fixed pictorially; and, from the picture, it may be produced again, long years after it was spoken.

Imagine your hearing once again the voices long hushed in death ! But memory is like this: it fixes all impressions and retains them; it never permits them to be destroyed, though it may not always be able to produce them instantly to a given call. Some memories are like well-classified libraries, in which you can readily discover even the smallest pamphlet; others are so confused that they are useless for practical purposes: yet even in these, nothing that ever came within their range has ever been lost; and whenever the right clue is presented, there is an immediate resurrection and recovery of sounds, and sights, and trains of thoughts long buried.

How terrible will it be, when the lost soul is met on the threshold of the dark world to which it goes, by the solemn words, " Son, remember ! " And what more fearful punishment could we imagine, than being compelled to meet again and to confront the hideous past, summoned by an inevitable remembrancer; whilst conscience, no longer stupefied and drugged, is sensitive enough to convince of the exceeding sinfulness of sin.

It is remarkable how different is the mental stimulus which is required by different castes of mind, to awaken dormant memories. In the case of some, the handwriting on an old letter, a picture, a scent borne on the breeze, a song, will be enough. Their own sorrow reminded Joseph's brethren of their disgraceful behaviour to their brother thirty years before. But in the case of the woman of Zarephath it was Elijah's holy life, combined with her own terrible sorrow. Beneath the spell of these two voices her memory gave up its dead, and her conscience was quickened into vigorous life. " Art thou come unto me to call my sin to remembrance ? "

Oh to live in the power of the Holy Ghost ! Our looks would sometimes then convict the stoutest sinners of sin;

as it is recorded of Finney, whose grieved face brought
conviction to a young woman, and through her to a whole
factory of operatives. Our holy walk would be a standing
rebuke; a mirror in which the sin-pocked might see the
ravages wrought by sin. Our words would then be sharp
two-edged swords, piercing to the dividing of the joints
and marrow, of soul and spirit.

And if any reader of this shall be conscious of some
hidden but unforgiven sin, let that one know that all
efforts to forget will some day be unavailing; sickness may
come, or bereavement, or bitter loss; and then that sin will
spring up, as if only committed yesterday, in all its horror
and agony. It is said that the spirit of the victim haunts the
murderer, until he makes reparation by confession and
surrender. There is some truth in it; for sin is only blotted
out of remembrance, both of God and the soul, when it has
been confessed, and put beneath the blood of Jesus. Confess your sin, and claim that cleansing now; and you will
hear the voice of God saying, " Your sins and iniquities
will I remember no more."

IV. ELIJAH TEACHES, LASTLY, THE SECRET OF GIVING LIFE.

It is a characteristic of those who are filled with the
Holy Ghost, that they carry with them everywhere the
spirit of life, even resurrection-life. We shall not only
convince men of sin; but we shall become channels through
which the Divine Life may enter them. Thus was it with
the prophet. But mark the conditions under which alone
we shall be able to fulfil this glorious function.

(1) *Lonely wrestlings.* " He took him out of her bosom,
and carried him up into a loft, where he abode, and laid
him upon his own bed. And he cried unto the Lord."
We are not specific enough in prayer; and we do not spend

enough time in intercession, dwelling with holy ardour on each beloved name, and on each heart-rending case. What wonder that we achieve so little!

(2) *Humility.* " He measured himself upon the child." How wonderful that so great a man should spend so much time and thought on that slender frame, and be content to bring himself into direct contact with that which might be thought to defile! It is a touching spectacle; but we must imitate it in some measure. We must seek the conversion of children, winning them ere Satan or the world attach them. But, to do so, we must stoop to them; becoming as little children to win little children for Jesus.

(3) *Perseverance.* " He measured himself three times, and cried unto the Lord." He was not soon daunted. It is thus that God tests the genuineness of our desire. These deferred answers lead us to lengths of holy boldness and pertinacity of which we should not otherwise have dreamed, but from which we shall never go back. " Men ought always to pray, and not to faint."

And his supplications met with the favour of God. " The Lord heard the voice of Elijah; and the soul of the child came into him again, and he revived." And as the prophet presented him to the grateful and rejoicing mother, he must have been beyond all things gratified with her simple testimony to the reality and power of the life which the Holy Ghost had begotten within him: " Now by this I know that thou art a man of God, and that the word of the Lord in thy mouth is truth." And what was the result of all? Simply this: that woman became so ennobled and changed by her contact with that man of God, that our Saviour awarded to her a prophet's reward (Matt. x. 41). Her work was small; her conceptions obscure; her home Gentile and heathen: and yet, because her motives were noble, and her spirit in sympathy with Elijah's, it was announced by Him, at whose bar we must all stand for our reward, that she had done what she could, and that her crown should shine as brightly as that placed on the brow of the prophet of God. We are rewarded, not according to our sphere, or the results of our work, but according to the sincerity and beauty of our motives; and these may be as lofty in an obscure widow as in Elijah himself.

VI

OBADIAH—A CONTRAST
(1 KINGS XVIII)

AFTER many days the word of the Lord again summoned Elijah to be on the move. Months, and even years, had passed in the retirement of Zarephath; the widow and her son had become bound to him by the most sacred ties; the humble home, with its loft and barrel of meal and cruse of oil, was hallowed with delightful memories of the un-failing carefulness of God.

It must have been a great trial for him to go; and how great was the contrast that awaited him ! He had probably heard of Ahab's search for him through all the neighbouring countries. There was not a nation or kingdom whither the incensed monarch had not sent to seek him, demanding an oath from the rulers that he was not in hiding there. It was not likely therefore that he would be received with much courtesy. Nay, the probability was that he would be instantly arrested; and perhaps put to torture to extort a revocation of the words which had placed the realm under the terrible interdict of drought. And as he contrasted the tumultuous roar of the waves foaming outside the harbour bar with the calm peace that reigned in the haven of rest, which had sheltered him so long, he might well have shrunk back in dismay. But he had no alternative but to go. He who had said, "Go hide thyself," now said, "Go show thyself." What was he but a servant, bound to obey ? And so, with the implicit obedience which has arrested our attention more than once, "Elijah went to show himself unto Ahab."

In this new departure the prophet evidently encouraged himself by the words on which he had leant when first he entered the monarch's presence, "The Lord of hosts liveth, before whom I stand" (1 Kings xviii. 15). And there may have rung through his spirit a refrain, throbbing with heroic faith, uttered centuries before by a kindred soul: "The Lord is my light and my salvation: whom shall I fear? the Lord is the strength of my life: of whom shall I be afraid? When the wicked, even mine enemies and my foes, came upon me to eat up my flesh, they stumbled and fell. Though an host should encamp against me, my heart shall not fear: though war should rise against me, in this will I be confident."

But, though Elijah's spirit was thus fortified against fear, it must have been very bitter to him to see the devastation which had been wrought in the land. The music of the brooklets was still. No green pastures carpeted the hills or vales. There was neither blossom on the fig-tree nor fruit in the vines; and the labour of the olive failed. The ground was chapt and barren. The hinds calved in the field, and deserted their young because there was no grass; and the wild asses, with distended nostrils, climbed the hills to snuff up the least breath of air that might allay the fever of their thirst. And, probably, the roads in the neighbourhood of the villages and towns were dotted by the stiffened corpses of the abject poor, who had succumbed to the severity of their privations. We have no idea, in these temperate regions, of the horrors of an Eastern drought. All this had been brought about instrumentally by the prophet's prayer; and it would have been intolerable, had he not eagerly hoped that his people would learn the exceeding sinfulness and evil of sin. "Thine own wickedness shall correct thee, and thy backslidings shall reprove thee; know, therefore, and see, that it is an evil thing and bitter, that thou hast forsaken the Lord thy God."

Though the famine was sore everywhere, it seems to have been most severe in Samaria. "There was a sore famine in Samaria." And it was this famine that brought out the true character of Ahab. We might have supposed that he would set himself to alleviate the miseries of his people; and, above all, that he would have turned back to God: but no—his one thought was about the horses and mules of his stud; and his only care was to save some of them alive. And so he starts on a mission, such as is still undertaken by the petty chieftains of Eastern tribes, to find grass. What selfishness is here! Mules and asses before his people! Seeking for grass, instead of seeking for God!

And yet such selfishness is as rife to-day as ever. Selfishness like this prompts the great ones of the earth to dash myriads of men against each other in the shock of battle, for the gratification of a mere personal *pique*, and regardless of the untold misery inflicted on thousands of hearts and homes. Selfishness like this makes men of wealth and fashion loll on beds of down; roll in luxurious carriages; and feast sumptuously every day—indifferent to the hopeless wretchedness of those who earn their wealth, and are paid a starvation wage. Selfishness like this still spends on an equipage, a horse, a dog, the keeping up of a shooting-box, the round of amusements, more than it can afford for the maintenance of God's work, or for the relief of the poor. Are professing Christians clear in this matter? Are there not many who spend as much on a single dinner party as they do on the needs of a dying world? And what is this but a repetition of the sin of Ahab, who went out to find grass for his beasts whilst his people were left to take their chance ! Oh that this spirit of selfishness were exorcised by the Spirit of Christ !—then missionary societies would not be hampered in their operations for want of funds; then the coffers of charitable institutions would be filled; then many a hard-working toiler would be able to give effect to schemes now blighted and arrested by the east wind of want. I do not blame Christian men for maintaining themselves in that position of life in which they were called; it is their apparent duty to retain that position as a sacred talent (1 Cor. vii. 20, 24). But I cannot understand a man daring to call himself a Christian and spending more upon the accessories and luxuries of his life than he does upon that service of man which is so dear to our Lord. This is surely the selfishness of Ahab.

It is startling to find such a man as OBADIAH occupying so influential a position at Ahab's court. "Obadiah was the governor (or steward) of his house." Now, according to his own testimony, Obadiah had feared the Lord from his youth (1 Kings xviii. 12). This is also the testimony of the sacred historian concerning him: "Obadiah feared the Lord greatly" (ver. 3). And he had given conspicuous proof of his piety; for, when Jezebel had swept the land with the besom of persecution, hunting down the prophets of the Lord, and consigning them to indiscriminate slaughter, he had rescued a hundred of the proscribed men, hiding them by fifty in a cave, and had fed them with bread and water. But though a good man, there was evidently a great lack of moral strength, of backbone, of vigorous life, in his character; otherwise he could never have held the position he did in the court of Ahab and Jezebel.

There is no possible harm in a Christian man holding a position of influence in a court or society where he can do so at no cost of principle. On the contrary, it may enable him to render priceless service to the cause of God. Where

would Luther and the Reformation have been, humanly
speaking, had it not been for the Elector of Saxony?
And what would have been the fate of our Wiclif, if John
o' Gaunt had not constituted him his ward? But very few
can occupy such a position, without putting kid on their
hands and velvet on their lips; without dropping something of their uncompromising speech; or dipping their
colours to the flag of expediency. And there is every
indication that this was the weak point with Obadiah.

Obadiah did not believe in carrying matters too far. Of
course, he could not fall in with this new order of things;
but then there was no need for him to force his religious
notions on every one. He was often shocked at what he
saw at court and found it hard to keep still: but then it
was no business of his; and it would not do to throw up
his situation, for he would be sure to lose it if he spoke
out. He was often sad at heart to witness the sufferings of
the prophets of the Lord, and half inclined to take up their
cause; but then a single man could not do much, and he
could, perhaps, help them better in a quiet way by keeping
where he was, though it might sometimes be a little strain
on his principles. The poor man must often have been in
a great strait to reconcile his duty to Jehovah with his duty
to his other master, Ahab. And Elijah shrewdly hinted at
it, when he said, "Go, tell *thy* lord—behold, Elijah is here!"
Imagine a courtier of Oliver Cromwell trying to be true to
the Commonwealth, and to the cause of the exiled Stuarts!
The life of policy and expediency is a species of rope-
walking—it needs considerable practice in the art of
balancing.

There are scores of Obadiahs everywhere around us,
and in the professing church. They know the right, and
are secretly trying to do it; but they say as little about
religion as they can. They never rebuke sin. They never

confess their true colours. They find pretexts and excuses to satisfy the remonstrances of an uneasy conscience. They are as nervous of being identified by declared Christians as Obadiah was when Elijah sent him to Ahab. They are sorry for those who suffer persecution for righteousness' sake; but it never occurs to them to stand in the pillory by their side. They content themselves with administering some little relief to them, as Obadiah did to the harried prophets; and, whilst they conceal that relief from the world, they put it in as a claim to the people of God for recognition and protection, as Obadiah did. "Was it not told my lord what I did ?" (1 Kings xviii. 13). They sometimes are on the point of throwing up all to take up an uncompromising attitude; but they find it hard to go forth to suffer affliction with the people of God, so long as they are well provided for within the palace walls.

What a contrast between Obadiah and Elijah ! And it is with the purpose of accentuating that contrast, and of bringing out into fuller relief the noble character of the prophet, that we have sought to elaborate this sketch of Ahab's steward.

I. THERE IS A CONTRAST BETWEEN THE INSIDE AND THE OUTSIDE OF THE CAMP FOR WITNESS-BEARING.

There is much said on both sides of the case. Many amongst us advise that the children of God should stay in the camp of the world—joining in its festivities; going to its places of amusement; taking the lead in its fashion and its course. In this way they hope to temper and steady it; to level it up; to make it Christian. It is a fair dream, exceedingly congenial to our natural tastes; and if it were only true, it would save a world of trouble. The poor prophets of the Lord might come back from their caves;

Elijah might become Ahab's vizier; and Obadiah's conscience might settle to rest. Indeed, Elijah's policy would be a supreme mistake; and we had better all become Obadiahs at once.

But there are two insurmountable difficulties in the way of our accepting this theory of levelling up from within.

(1) *It is in direct opposition to the teaching of Scripture.* "Come out from her, my people," is the one summons that rings like a clarion note from board to board. "Come out from among them and be ye separate, saith the Lord; and touch not the unclean thing." There is not a single hero or saint, whose name sparkles on the inspired page, who moved his times from within: all, without exception, have raised the cry, "Let us go forth without the camp"; and have joined the constant stream of martyrs, confessors, prophets, and saints, of whom the world was not worthy, but who can trace their kinship to Him of whom it is written, "He suffered without the gate." The only Scriptural course for God's witness-bearers is to go out to Him without the camp. In the world, but not of it. Wearing the pilgrim garb, manifesting the pilgrim spirit, uttering the pilgrim confession.

(2) *This theory will not work.* The man who goes into the world to level it up will soon find himself levelled down. Was not this the case with Obadiah? Instead of getting Ahab to think with himself, Ahab sent him unto all fountains of water and unto all brooks, to find grass for his horses and mules. Surely this was a miserable errand for one who feared the Lord greatly! But this is only a sample of the kind of things which must be borne and done by such as try to serve two masters. Compare the influence exerted on the behalf of Sodom by Abraham, on the heights

of Mamre, with that of Lot, who, not content with pitching his tent towards the city gate, went to live inside, and even became one of the aldermen of the place (Gen. xix. 1). Remember that Lot was carried captive in the sack of Sodom; but Abraham rescued him. But why need we multiply instances ? This matter is undergoing daily proof. The Christian woman who marries an ungodly man is in imminent danger of being soon dragged down to his level. The servant of God who enters into partnership with a man of the world cannot keep the business from drifting. The church which admits the world into its circle will find that it will get worldly quicker than the world will become Christian.

The safest and strongest position is outside the camp. Archimedes said that he could move the world, if only he had a point of rest given him outside it. Thus, too, can a handful of God's servants influence their times, if only they resemble Elijah, whose life was spent altogether outside the pale of the court and the world of his time.

II. THERE IS A CONTRAST BETWEEN PREVENTIVE AND AGGRESSIVE GOODNESS.

Obadiah sought simply to prevent a great harm being done. He shielded the prophets from the sword of Jezebel, and from the touch of famine. And this was well. Preventive goodness like this serves a very useful purpose. It rears Homes, and Refuges, and bulwarks of defence, behind which persecuted and threatened lives may thrive. But, after all, the world needs something more. It is not enough to deal with the poisoned streams; a hand is needed to cast the healing salt into the fountain-head. There is an urgent demand for men like Elijah and John the Baptist, who dare oppose the perpetrators of evil deeds, and arraign them before the bar of God, and compel them to bow before the offended majesty of a broken law.

For this there is needed a positive enduement of power, which cannot be had by the half-hearted; but is the glad prerogative of those who, from the crown of the head to the sole of the foot, are servants of God. Obadiah had no power of this kind. How could he have? On the other hand, Elijah was full of it; and, because he was so, he succeeded in arresting the tides of sin when they were in full flood.

It is not enough to shelter the prophets; we must go and show ourselves to Ahab. We may be as sugar; but we must also be like salt, that stays the progress of consumption. The preventive and ameliorative, the healing agencies are good; but the aggressive are better still, because they deal with the hidden causes of things. May God send to His Church a handful of lion-like men, like Elijah, of whom this is the majestic record: "Elijah went to show himself unto Ahab"; to confront the royal culprit, to lay the king under arrest.

III. THERE IS A CONTRAST BETWEEN THE CAUTION OF EXPEDIENCY AND THE FEARLESSNESS OF FAITH.

When Elijah told Obadiah to tell his master that he was awaiting him, the astonished courtier was incredulous. He knew how irritated and incensed Ahab had been, and that his anger was at white heat still; and it seemed madness for the prophet to expose himself to its flames. Indeed, he thought either that the prophet did not know the way in which the king had sought for him; or that the Spirit of the Lord would carry him off before they could meet. It never occurred to him that Elijah dare meet the king if he really knew how matters stood. And even supposing that *he* were foolhardy enough to adventure himself, surely God would prevent him from stepping into the lion's lair. In any case, he wished to have nothing to do with it. He was more anxious for himself than for the work of God, or the wishes of Elijah. Twice over he repeated the words, "he shall slay me." And it was only when Elijah appealed to God as the witness of his solemn oath, and assured him that he would surely show himself to Ahab ere the sun went down, that he reluctantly went to meet Ahab and told him. How unable he was to form a true conception of the fearlessness of Elijah !

And what was the source of that fearlessness ? Surely it is unfolded to us in the words of Elijah's sublime asseveration: "The Lord of hosts liveth, before whom I stand." God was more real to Elijah than Ahab. He was a courtier in the throne-room of the King of kings. How could he be afraid of a man that should die, and of the son of man that should become as the grass of the mower's scythe, withered by the noontide heat ? The fear of God had made him impervious to all other fear. Faith sees the mountain full of horses and chariots of fire. Faith can hear the tread of twelve legions of angels marshalling for its defence. Faith can detect the outlines of those Almighty hands which hide the children of God in their hollow. And so, with unblanched face and undismayed heart, God's Elijahs go on to do His commands, though their way is blocked by as many devils as there are tiles upon the housetops. The Obadiahs assert that they will never dare to carry their proposals through; but they live to see their predictions falsified, and their mean suggestions shamed.

IV. There is a contrast between the reception given to these two types of character by the ungodly.

Ahab could tolerate Obadiah, because he never rebuked him. When salt has lost its savour it does not sting, though it be rubbed into an open wound. But as soon as Ahab saw Elijah, he accosted him as the great troubler of the time. "It came to pass, when Ahab saw Elijah, that Ahab said unto him, Is it thou, thou troubler of Israel?" (ver. 17, R.V.). Years after, speaking of another devoted servant of God, whose advice was demanded by Jehoshaphat, this same Ahab said, "I hate him; for he doth not prophesy good concerning me, but evil."

There is no higher testimony to the consistency of our life than the hearty hatred of the Ahabs around us. One of the most scathing condemnations that could be pronounced on men is contained in those terrible words of our Lord: "*The world cannot hate you*; but Me it hateth, because I testify of it, that the works thereof are evil." Who would not undergo all the hate that the Ahabs can heap on us, rather than incur that sentence from the lips of Christ! "Blessed are ye, when men shall revile you, and persecute you, and shall say all manner of evil against you falsely, for My sake. Rejoice, and be exceeding glad." If all men speak well of you, you may begin to question whether you are not becoming mere Obadiahs. But if Ahab accuses you of troubling him, rejoice; and tell him to his face that his troubles is due to a broken commandment, and to the idols before which he bows. If there should read these lines those who are in trouble, enduring affliction, their life smitten with drought—let them ask whether the cause is not to be found in broken vows, in desecrated temples, in forfeited oaths. If so, return at once, with tears of penitence and words of confession, unto the Lord.

"He hath torn, and He will heal; He hath smitten, and He will bind up."

There, face to face, we leave Ahab and Elijah. We need not ask which is the more royal of the two; nor need we spend our time in looking for Obadiah. We cannot but admire the noble bearing of the prophet of God. But let us remember it was due, not to his inherent character, but to his faith. "By faith he quenched the violence of fire, escaped the edge of the sword, out of weakness was made strong, stopped the mouth of this lion." And if we will acquire a similar faith, we may anticipate similar results on the meaner platform of our own lives.

VII

THE PLAN OF CAMPAIGN
(1 KINGS XVIII)

WHEN Elijah left Zarephath, it is more than probable that his mind was utterly destitute of any fixed plan of action. He knew that he must show himself to Ahab; and that rain was not far away: for these were his definite marching orders—"Go, show thyself unto Ahab; and I will send rain upon the earth." But more than that he knew not. There may have flitted before his spirit dim previsions of that sublime conflict on Carmel's heights, but he knew nothing certainly; his one endeavour was to quiet his eager nature, like a weaned child, hushing it with the lullaby of an old refrain: "My soul, wait thou only upon God, for my expectation is from Him."

The plan of this great campaign for God against Baal, for truth against error, may have been revealed to Elijah on his journey from Zarephath to find Ahab; and at a sudden glance, as when a lightning-flash reveals to a benighted traveller the winding pathway he must follow through the vale beneath. But it is quite as likely that it was revealed in pieces, like the separate bits of a children's puzzle—handed out, one by one, from the parent to the child, who might be confused to do with more than one at a time. This is so often God's way; and they who trust Him utterly are quite pleased to have it so. There is even a novelty and beauty in life, when every step is unforeseen and unexpected, and opens up new vistas of loveliness in God's management and in Himself.

If we seek to think ourselves into Elijah's attitude of heart and mind, as he left the shelter of Zarephath, and began to pass through the incidents that culminated in Carmel, it seems to have been threefold. And surely it is of surpassing interest to learn how such a man felt, as he approached the sublime crisis of his life.

I. HE WAS FILLED WITH A CONSUMING PASSION FOR THE GLORY OF GOD.

"Let it be known that Thou art God in Israel." This prayer is the key to his heart. He neither knew nor cared to know what would become of himself; but his soul was on fire with a holy jealousy for the glory of God. He could not bear to think of those wrecked altars or martyred prophets. He could not bear to think how the Land of Promise was groaning beneath the obscene and deadly rites of Phœnician idolatry. He could not bear to think that his people were beginning to imagine that the God of Abraham, of Isaac, and of Israel had abdicated in favour of these false deities brought newly in. And when he was compelled to face these things, his spirit was stirred to its depths with indignation and sorrow.

Well would it be if each one of us were similarly inspired! We are very eager for the success of *our* work, *our* church, *our* sect. If these thrive, we are satisfied; if these languish, we are depressed. We are wholly occupied with the interests of our own tiny pools, oblivious of the great sea of divine glory lying near by, in perpetual sunshine. Is it wonderful that we have so small a measure of success? God will not give His glory to another, nor His praise to the graven images of our own conceit. But in this, also, God is willing to lift our daily experience to the level of our loftiest ideals. Only trust Him to do it; ask and expect Him to fill you with the fire of that zeal which burnt in the heart of Elijah, consuming all that was base, corrupt, and selfish, and making the whole man a fit agent for God. This was no indigenous growth. It was not more natural to him than it is to any one of us. It was simply one of the fruits of the indwelling of the Holy Ghost, who is equally promised to the most ignoble nature.

II. HE WAS PROFOUNDLY CONVINCED THAT HE WAS ONLY A SERVANT.

"Let it be known that Thou art God in Israel; *and that I am Thy servant.*" It was not for the slave in olden times to originate, or scheme, or plan; but to be pliant to the least expression of the master's will—to be a tool in his hand, a chess-piece on the board for him to move just where he willed. And this was the attitude of Elijah's spirit—surrendered, yielded, emptied; plastic to the hands that reach down out of heaven moulding men.

This attitude is the true one for us all. Are we not too fond of doing things for God, instead of letting God do what He chooses through us ? We say, "We will go yonder; we will do this and that; we will work for God thus." We do not consider that we should first inquire if this were God's will for us. We do not recognize His absolute ownership. We often miss doing what He sorely wants to do, because we insist on carrying out some little whim of our own. This is the blight on much of the activity of Christian people at the present time. They are not satisfied to be as the Apostle Paul was, "the slave of Jesus Christ" (Rom. i. 1, marg.).

III. ELIJAH WAS EAGERLY DESIROUS TO KNOW AND WORK OUT GOD'S PLAN.

"Let it be known this day that Thou art God in Israel; and that I am Thy servant; and *that I have done all these things according to Thy word.*" When once a man feels that he is working out God's plan, and that God is working out His plan through him, he is invincible. Men, circumstances, opposition, are of no more account than the chaff of the autumn threshings. God's plan is His purpose; and God's purpose shall be accomplished, though earth and heaven pass away. And this was doubtless one element in Elijah's splendid strength.

This question as to our relation to God's plan is most important. Because the power and blessing of God are only to be enjoyed, in all their fulness, by those who are where He would have them be. God had the plan of the desert wanderings in His thought long before Israel left Egypt; and He worked out that plan by the movements of the cloud over the desert sands. The manna fell on any given morning, only where the cloud was brooding, shielding the host by its fleecy folds. To get the manna and the shade, the blood-redeemed must be just where God's plan required them to be. This is a parable of our lives. Would we have Divine supplies? We must keep step with the Divine plan. The fire burns only when we erect the altar according to God's word. We must not be disobedient to a heavenly vision. We must not spend our years in day dreams, or in seeking comfort; but must be incessant in uttering the cry, "What wilt Thou have me to do?"

There are many ways of learning God's plan. Sometimes it is revealed *in circumstances*—not always pleasant; but ever acceptable, because revealing our Father's will. No circumstance happens outside His permission; and therefore each is a King's messenger, bearing His message, though we are sometimes puzzled to decipher it. Sometimes God's plan is revealed *by strong impressions of duty*, which increase in proportion as they are prayed over, and are tested by the Word of God.

There are many voices by which God can speak His will to the truly surrendered spirit. If there is any confusion as to what it is, it is due to one of these two causes: either the will is not fully yielded to do God's will, so soon as known, but there is some film between the two, preventing the entire permeation of the human by the Divine; or the time of perfect knowledge has not arrived, and we must be content quietly to wait for the salvation of God. It is a true rule for us all, to do nothing, so long as we are in any uncertainty; but to examine ourselves, and to be ready to act so soon as we know. We may not infrequently have the experience of the Apostle Peter repeated in our own: "While Peter doubted in himself what this vision, which he had seen, should mean, behold, the men sent from Cornelius stood before the gate" (Acts x. 17). The knocking of three men at a gate may sometimes indicate God's plan; or a dream from across the sea; or the glimpse of a weary face, just a little more weary than others around. (Acts xvi. 9, 10; John v. 6, 7.)

The plan, as Elijah unfolded it to Ahab, was eminently adapted to the circumstances of the case. All Israel was to be gathered by royal summons to Carmel, which reared itself above the plain of Esdraelon, a noble site for a national meeting-ground. Special care was to be taken to secure the presence of the representatives of the systems that had dared to rival the worship of Jehovah; "the prophets of Baal four hundred and fifty, and the prophets of the Asherah four hundred, which eat at Jezebel's table."

A test was then to be imposed on these rival systems, which the adherents of Baal could not possibly refuse; for he was the Sun-god, and this was a trial by fire.

Elijah knew that the altar of Baal would remain smokeless. He was equally sure that Jehovah would answer his faith by fire, as He had done again and again in the glorious past. He felt convinced also that the people, unable to escape the evidence of their senses, would for ever disavow the accursed systems of Phoenicia, and would return once more to the worship of the God of their fathers.

It is probable that, in the case of Ahab, only so much of this plan was disclosed as was necessary to secure the gathering of the people. To tell him too much would be to invite criticism, and perhaps to arouse opposition. It is not likely that he would have been so pliant, unless allured by the bait of rain. " So Ahab sent unto all the children of Israel, and gathered the prophets together unto Mount Carmel."

We do not know how this was done; but doubtless the royal word would be passed through the country by a system of messengers, like those which once gave warning of the peril of Jabesh-Gilead; or, in later times, carried through the Highlands the fiery cross. But in any case this summoning of the people must have taken a few days. And it is by that interval of waiting that we are for a moment arrested. It was like the sultry hush which precedes the breaking of a tropic thunderstorm; or the momentary pause before long lines of armed men are launched at each other in the shock of battle.

Where and how did Elijah spend that interval ? We are told that " he *came* unto all the people," when they were finally assembled on the appointed day. We may not press the word; but does it not suggest that he came from the contrary direction to that from which the people gathered ? And if the people came from the whole circumference of the land, may he not have come from some ancient cave of Carmel's heights, just where the long range of hills drops suddenly down in sheer precipices on the sea ?

In my opinion, Elijah spent those memorable days of waiting on Carmel itself; sheltering himself and the lad in some wild cave at night, and by day going carefully over the scene of the approaching conflict. How mournfully would he bend over the stones of that altar, which was broken down!—broken down not by the wild weather, or the devastating hand of time; but by the wicked behest of Jezebel (1 Kings xviii. 32). How eagerly would he search out the original twelve stones, strewn recklessly afar, and covered by wild undergrowth. He would need them soon! How constantly would he stay himself upon his God, and pour out litanies of supplication for the people, and gird himself for the coming conflict by effectual fervent prayer. Would he not learn the way down to Kishon's brook beneath, and visit the perennial spring, from which he would fill the barrels again and yet again with water!

We sometimes seem to think that that answer of fire was probably so much the result of God's determination as to have been largely independent of any special exercise of the prophet's faith. We suppose that more faith and prayer were needed to bring the *rain* than to bring the leaping, consuming *flame*. We consider that the one needed the intense sevenfold prayer; whilst the other needed only the few sentences spoken in the audience of the amazed people, at the moment of sacrifice. But this is a very superficial reading of the story; and it is not in harmony with the general dealings of God. " For all these things I will be inquired of." As much fervent believing prayer was needed for the fire as for the rain;

and the answer by fire would never have come that day, if the previous days had not been spent in the presence-chamber of God. The prayer during ten days of waiting, in the upper room, must precede the descent of the Holy Ghost, as a baptism of fire, on the Day of Pentecost.

It is a sublime spectacle—this yielded, surrendered man, awaiting on Carmel, in steadfast faith, the gathering of the people, and the unfolding of the.purpose of God. He had no fear about the issue; and as the days rolled by, his soul rose in higher and ever higher joy. He expected soon to see a nation at the feet of God.

And he was all this, not because he was of a different make to ourselves; but because he had got into the blessed habit of dealing with God at first hand, as a Living Reality, in whose presence it was his privilege and glory always to stand.

VIII

The Conflict on the Heights of Carmel
(1 Kings xviii)

It is early morning upon Mount Carmel. We are standing on the highest point, looking northwards to where Hermon, on the extreme borders of the land, rears its snow-capped head to heaven. Around us on the left lies the Mediterranean Sea; its deep blue waters flecked here and there by the sails of the Tyrian mariners. Immediately at Carmel's base winds Kishon's ancient brook, once choked by the slaughter of Sisera's host; and beyond it stretches the plain of Esdraelon, the garden of Palestine, but now sere and barren with three years' drought. Away there in the distance is the city of Jezreel, with the royal palace and the idol distinctly visible.

From all sides the crowds are making their way towards this spot, which, from the remotest times, has been associated with worship. No work is being done anywhere; the fires are dying out in the smithy and the forge; the instruments of labour hang useless on the walls; and the whole thought of young and old is concentrated on that mighty convocation to which Ahab has summoned them. See how the many thousands of Israel are slowly gathering, and taking up every spot of vantage ground from which a view can be obtained of the proceedings; and prepared for any extreme—from the impure rites of Baal and Astarte, to the re-establishment of their fathers' religion on the dead bodies of the false priests!

The people are nearly gathered, and there is the regular

tread of marshalled men; four hundred prophets of Baal, conspicuous with the sun-symbols flashing on their brows; but the prophets of Astarte are absent: the queen, at whose table they ate, has overruled the summons of the king. And now, through the crowd, the litter of the king, borne by stalwart carriers, threads its way, surrounded by the great officers of state.

But our thought turns from the natural panorama, and the sea of upturned faces, and the flashing splendour of the priests, sure of court favour, and insolently defiant. And we fix our thought with intense interest on that one man, of sinewy build and flowing hair, who, with flashing eye and compressed lip, awaits the quiet hush which will presently fall upon that mighty concourse. One man against a nation! See, with what malignant glances his every movement is watched by the priests. No tiger ever watched its victim more fiercely! If they may have their way, he will never touch yonder plain again.

The king alternates between fear and hate; but restrains himself, because he feels that, somehow, the coming of the rain depends on this one man. And through the crowd, if there be sympathisers, they are hushed and still. Even Obadiah discreetly keeps out of the way. But do not fear for Elijah—he needs no sympathy! He is consciously standing in the presence of One to whom the nations of men are as grasshoppers. All heaven is at his back. Legions of angels fill the mountain with horses and chariots of fire. He is only a man of like passions with ourselves, but he is full of faith and spiritual power; he has learnt the secret of moving God Himself; he can avail himself of the very resources of Deity, as a slender rod may draw lightning from the cloud. This very day, by faith—not by any inherent power, but by faith—you shall see him subdue a kingdom; work righteousness; escape the edge of the

sword; wax valiant in the fight; and turn to flight armies
of the aliens. Nothing shall be impossible to him. Is it not
written that " all things are possible to him that believeth?"
He spoke seven times during the course of that memorable
day; and his words are the true index of what was passing
in his heart.

I. ELIJAH UTTERED A REMONSTRANCE.

" Elijah came unto all the people and said, How long
halt ye between two opinions? If Jehovah be God, follow
Him; but if Baal, then follow him." To his clear faith,
which was almost sight, there was no " if." He did not
doubt for a moment that Jehovah was God. But he
wanted to show the people the absurdity of their position.
Religions so diametrically opposed could not both be
right. One of them must be wrong; and as soon as the
true one was discovered, the other, shown to be false,
must be cast to the winds.

At present their position was illogical and absurd. Their
course was like the limp of a man whose legs are uneven;
or like the device of a servant employed to serve two
masters—doing his best for both, and failing to please
either. His sincere and simple soul had no patience with
such egregious folly. No doubt they had drifted into it;
as men often do into absurd and wrong positions. We are
all liable to that drift of the stream. But the time had
come for the nation to be arrested in its attempt to mingle
the worship of Jehovah and of Baal; and compelled to
choose between the two issues that presented themselves.
Undoubtedly, the prophet felt that if once his people were
compelled to choose between the two, and to say whether
the Jehovah of their fathers, or Baal, should be God, there
could be no doubt as to their verdict.

The people seemed to have been stunned and ashamed that such alternatives should be presented to their choice; for "they answered him not a word." Oh for the clearsightedness of that faith which shall show men the unreasonableness of their position—sweeping away the cobwebs of sophistry with a single movement of the hand; and arraigning them at the bar of their own consciences, silent and condemned. It is needed in our day as much as ever. Everywhere men are trying to win the smile of the world, and the "well-done" of Christ. They crowd alike the temples of mammon and of God. They try to be popular in the court of Saul, and to stand well with the exiled David.

II. ELIJAH THREW DOWN A CHALLENGE.

"The God that answereth by fire, let Him be God." It was a fair proposal; because Baal was the lord of the sun, and the god of those productive natural forces of which heat is the element and sign. The votaries of Baal could not therefore refuse.

And every Israelite could recall many an occasion in the glorious past when Jehovah had answered by fire. It burnt in the acacia bush, which was its own fuel; it shone like a beacon-light in the van of the desert march; it gleamed on the brow of Sinai; it smote the murmuring crowds; it fell upon the sacrifices which awaited it on the brazen altar. It was the emblem of Jehovah, and the sign of His acceptance of His people's service.

When Elijah, therefore, proposed that each side should offer a bullock, and await an answer by fire, he secured the immediate acquiescence of the people. "All the people answered and said, It is well spoken."

That proposal was made in the perfect assurance that

God would not fail him. Had he not spent days in prayer? Had not the Divine plan been revealed to him? Was it to be supposed for a moment that God would push His servant into the front of the battle, and then leave him? Granted that a miracle must be wrought ere the sun set: there was no difficulty about that to a man who lived in the secret place of the Most High. Miracles are only the results of the higher laws of His presence-chamber.

God will never fail the man who trusts Him utterly. He may keep him waiting till the fourth watch of the morning; but the grey dawn will reveal Him stepping across the billows' crests to His servant's help. Be sure that you are on God's plan; then forward in God's name!—the very elements shall obey you, and fire shall leap from heaven at your command.

III. Elijah dealt out withering sarcasm.

For the first time in their existence, the false priests were unable to insert the secret spark of fire among the faggots that lay upon their altar. They were compelled, therefore, to rely on a direct appeal to their patron deity. And this they did with might and main. Round and round the altar they went in the mystic choric dance, breaking their rank sometimes by an excited leap up and down at the altar which was made; and all the while repeating the monotonous chant, " Baal, hear us! Hear us, Baal! " But there was no voice, nor any that answered. " Their idols are silver and gold, the work of men's hands. They have mouths, but they speak not; eyes have they, but they see not; they have ears, but they hear not; they that make them are like them, so is every one that trusteth in them."

Three hours passed thus. Their deity slowly drove his golden car up the steep of heaven, and ascended his throne in the zenith. It was surely the time of his greatest power, and he must help them then, if ever. But all he did was to bronze to a deeper tint the eager, upturned faces of his priests.

Elijah could ill conceal his delight in their defeat. He knew it would be so. He was so sure that nothing could avert their utter discomfiture, that he could afford to mock them, by suggesting a cause for the indifference of their god: " Cry aloud, for he is a god; either he is talking, or he is pursuing, or he is in a journey, or peradventure he sleepeth, and must be awaked." Sarcasm is an invaluable weapon when it is used to expose the ridiculous pretensions of error, and to convince men of the folly and unreasonableness of their ways.

" And they cried aloud; and cut themselves after their manner, with knives and lancets, till their blood gushed out upon them." Surely their extremity was enough to touch the compassion of any deity, however hard to move ! And, since the heavens still continued dumb, did it not prove to the people that their religion was a delusion and a sham ?

Thus three more hours passed by, till the hour had come when, in the temple of Jerusalem, the priests of God were accustomed to offer the evening lamb. " But there was neither voice, nor any to answer, nor any that regarded." The altar stood cold and smokeless, the bullock unconsumed.

IV. ELIJAH ISSUED AN INVITATION.

His time had come at last; and his first act was to invite the people nearer. He knew what his faith and prayer had won from God; but he wanted the answer of fire to be beyond dispute. He therefore invited the close scrutiny of the people, as he reared the broken altar of the Lord. As he sought, with reverent care, those scattered stones; and built them together so that the twelve stood as one— meet symbol of the unity of the ideal Israel in the sight of God—the keen glances of the people, in his close proximity, could see that there was no inserted torch or secret spark.

Do we not want a few more, who, amid the scatterings of the present day, can still discern the true unity of the Church, the body of Christ ? We may never see that unity visibly manifested until we see the Bride, the Lamb's wife, descend out of heaven from God, having the glory of God. But nevertheless we can enter into God's ideal of it as a spiritual unity, existing unbroken in His thought, and unaffected by the divisions of our times. Is it not clear that, during this age, the Church of Christ was never meant to be a visible corporate body, but to be a great spiritual reality, consisting of all faithful and loyal spirits, in all communions, who, holding the Head, are necessarily one with each other ?

V. ELIJAH GAVE A COMMAND.

His faith was exuberant. He was so sure of God, that he dared to heap difficulties in his way, knowing that there is no real difficulty for infinite power. The more unlikely the answer was, the more glory would there be to God. Oh, matchless faith ! which can laugh at impossibilities, and can even heap them one upon another, to have the pleasure of seeing God vanquish them—as a steam hammer cracks a nut-shell placed under it by the wondering child.

The altar was reared; the wood laid in order; the bullock cut in pieces: but to prevent any possibility of

fraud, and to make the coming miracle still more wonderful, Elijah said, " Fill four barrels with water, and pour it
on the sacrifice and on the wood." This they did three
times, till the wood was drenched, and the water filled the
trench, making it impossible for a spark to travel across.

Alas, few of us have faith like this! We are not so sure
of God that we dare to pile difficulties in His way. We
all try our best to make it easy for Him to help us.
Yet what this man had, we too may have, by prayer and
fasting.

VI. ELIJAH OFFERED A PRAYER.

Such a prayer! It was quiet and assured, confident of
an answer. Its chief burden was that God should vindicate
Himself that day, in showing Himself to be God indeed,
and in turning the people's heart back to Himself.

Whenever we can so lose ourselves in prayer as to forget
personal interest, and to plead for the glory of God, we
have reached a vantage ground from which we can win
anything from Him. Our blessed Lord, in His earthly life,
had but one passion—that His Father might be glorified;
and now He cannot resist fulfilling the prayer which
advances this as its plea: " Whatsoever ye shall ask the
Father in My name, that will I do; that *the Father may be
glorified* in the Son."

Is it wonderful that " the fire of the Lord fell, and con-
sumed the burnt sacrifice, and the wood, and the stones,
and the dust, and licked up the water that was in the
trench "? It could not have been otherwise! And let us
not think that this is an old-world tale, never to be repeated. The fire still waits for the Promethean faith that
can bring it down. If there were the same need, and if any
one of us exercised the same faith, we might again see fire

descending. Did not the Holy Ghost inaugurate this very age with flames of fire ? Our God is a consuming fire; and when once the unity of His people is recognized, and His presence is sought, He will descend, overcoming all obstacles, and converting a drenched and dripping sacrifice into food on which He Himself can feed.

VII. ELIJAH ISSUED AN ORDER FOR EXECUTION.

It was a very terrible act; and yet what could he do ? The saints of those times knew nothing of our false notions of liberality. Tell Elijah that those men might be sincere, he would find it difficult to believe it; and he would assert that they were none the less dangerous to the best interest of his people. To let them escape would be to licence them as the agents of apostasy. They must die. And so the order went forth from those stern lips: " Take the prophets of Baal, let not one of them escape." The people were in the mood to obey. Only a moment before they had rent the air with the shout, " Jehovah, He is the God! Jehovah He is the God! " They see how hideously they had been deceived. And now they close round the cowed and vanquished priests, who see that resistance is in vain, and that their hour is come.

" And they took them." Some took one, and some another; each priest was hurried down the mountain-side by the frenzied and determined men who were beginning to see in them the cause of the long-continued drought.

" Elijah brought them down to the brook Kishon, and slew them there." One after another they fell beneath his sword; whilst the king stood by, a helpless spectator of their doom, and Baal did nought to save them.

And when the last was dead, the prophet knew that rain was not far off. He could almost hear the footfall of the clouds hurrying up towards the land. He knew, what we all need to know, that God Himself can only bless the land or heart which no longer shelters within its borders rivals to Himself. May God clear us of His rivals, and impart to us Elijah's faith, that we may also be strong and do exploits!

IX

Rain at Last !
(1 Kings xviii)

We can in a very inadequate degree realize the horrors of an Eastern drought. And it would have been difficult in the parched land on which Elijah gazed from Carmel, to have recognized that garden of the Lord of which Moses said: " The Lord thy God giveth thee a good land; a land full of brooks of water, of rivers and depths, which spring out of valleys and hills; a land wherein thou shalt eat bread without scarceness, and in which thou shalt not lack anything."

But beside this exquisite delineation, there had been given to Moses a description of the certain calamities that would ensue if Israel went aside from any of the words which God commanded, to the right hand, or to the left. And amongst other items of misery, it was expressly stated that the heaven overhead should be brass, and the earth underfoot iron; and that the very rain should be transformed to powder and dust (Deut. xxviii. 23, 24). This terrible prediction had now been literally fulfilled. And the anguish of the land was directly attributable to the apostasy of its people. All this was the result of sin. The iniquities of Israel had separated between them and their God, and Elijah knew this right well; and this prompted him to act the part of executioner to the priests of Baal, who had been the ringleaders in the national revolt from God, but whose bodies now lay in ghastly death on the banks of the Kishon, or were being hurried out to sea.

Ahab must have stood by Elijah in the Kishon gorge, and been an unwilling spectator of that fearful deed of vengeance; not daring to resist the outburst of popular indignation, or to attempt to shield the men whom he had himself encouraged and introduced. When the last priest had bitten the dust, Elijah turned to the king, and said, " Get thee up, eat and drink; for there is a sound of abundance of rain." It was as if he said, " Get thee up to where thy tents are pitched on yon broad upland sweep; the feast is spread in thy gilded pavilion; thy lackeys await thee; feast thee on thy dainties; but be quick! for now that the land is rid of these traitor priests, and God is once more enthroned in His rightful place, the showers of rain cannot be longer delayed. Can you not hear the sough of the western breeze, which shall soon become a rain-bearing hurricane? Be quick! or the rain may interrupt thy carouse."

What a contrast between these two men! " Ahab went up to eat and drink. And Elijah went up to the top of Carmel; and he cast himself down upon the earth, and put his face between his knees." It is no more than we might have expected of the king. When his people were suffering the extremities of drought, he cared only to find grass enough to save his stud; and now, though his faithful priests had died by hundreds, he thought only of the banquet that awaited him in his pavilion. Cruel, cowardly, mean, and sensual, are the least epithets we can apply to this worthless man, clad though he was with the royal robes of Israel. I think I can see Ahab and Elijah ascending those heights together: no sympathy; no common joy; no reciprocated thanksgiving. The king turns straight off to his tents; whilst the servant of God climbs steadily up to the highest part of the mountain, and finds an oratory at the base of a yet higher spur, or promontory, from which

a marvellous view could be obtained of the broad expanse
of the Mediterranean, which slept under the growing
stillness of the coming night.

Such contrasts still reveal themselves. Crises reveal the
secrets of men's hearts, and show of what stuff they are
made. The children of this world will spend their days in
feasting, and their nights in revelry, though a world is
rushing down to ruin. If only they can eat and drink, they
are regardless of the needs of the perishing, and the judgments of God. Such feasted with Belshazzar when the foe
was at the gates of Babylon; and such filled with their
frivolities the royal apartments of Whitehall when William
of Orange was landing at Tor Bay. And woe to the land
when such men rule! The sequence between the sensual
luxury of the rulers and the decadence of the nation was
well pointed out by Isaiah when he said:—" Woe unto
them that rise up early in the morning, that they may
follow strong drink; that tarry late into the night, till wine
inflame them! And the harp and the lute, the tabret and
the pipe, and wine, are in their feasts: but they regard not
the work of the Lord, neither have they considered the
operation of His hands. Therefore my people are gone
into captivity " (Isa. v. 11–13 R.V.). May our beloved
country be preserved from having such leaders as these!
And may our youth be found, not garlanded and scented
for the Ahab feasts, but with Elijah on the bleak uplands;
where there may be no dainty viands, but where the air is
fresh, and life is free, and the spirit is braced to noble
deeds.

THERE ARE CERTAIN CHARACTERISTICS IN ELIJAH'S PRAYER,
WHICH WE MUST NOTICE AS WE PASS; BECAUSE THEY SHOULD
FORM PART OF ALL TRUE PRAYER.

(1) *It was based on the promise of God*

When Elijah was summoned from Zarephath to resume
his public work, his marching orders were capped by the
specific promise of rain: "Go, show thyself unto Ahab;
and I will send rain on the earth." To natural reason this
might have seemed to render prayer unnecessary. Would
not God fulfil His promise, and send the rain, altogether
irrespectively of further prayer? But Elijah's spiritual
instincts argued otherwise, and more truly. Though he had
never heard the words, yet he anticipated the thought of a
later prophet, who, after enunciating all that God was
prepared to do for His people, uttered these significant
words: "Thus saith the Lord God, I will yet for this be
inquired of by the house of Israel, to do it for them."

God's promises are given, not to restrain, but to incite to
prayer. They show the direction in which we may ask,
and the extent to which we may expect an answer. They
are the mould into which we may pour our fervid spirits
without fear. They are the signed cheque, made payable to
order, which we must endorse and present for payment.
Though the Bible be crowded with golden promises from
board to board, yet will they be inoperative, until we turn
them into prayer. It is not our province to argue the
reasonableness of this; it is enough to accentuate and
enforce it. Why should it not be sufficient to silence all
questions by saying, that we have here reached one of the
primal laws of the spiritual world, as simple, as certain, as
universal, as any that obtain in the world of nature?
Promises of abundant harvest smile to the husbandman
from earth and sky: but he knows that they will not be

realized unless he puts into operation the laws and processes of agriculture; and as he does so, it is not necessary for his success that he should understand the why and wherefore; it is enough for him to do his little part, and he finds that every promise is fulfilled in the produce shed at his feet from Nature's golden horn.

When, therefore, we are asked *why* men should pray, and *how* prayer avails, we are not careful to answer more than this: "Prayer is the instinct of the religious life; it is one of the first principles of the spiritual world." It is clearly taught in the Word of God to be prevalent with the Almighty. It has been practised by the noblest and saintliest of men, who have testified to its certain efficacy. Our Lord Jesus not only practised it, but proclaimed its value in words which have been plunged a myriad times into the crucible of experience, and are as true to-day as ever: "Ask, and it shall be given you; seek, and ye shall find; knock, and it shall be opened unto you." We are content, therefore, to pray, though we are as ignorant of the philosophy of the *modus operandi* of prayer, as we are of any natural law. We find it no dreamy reverie or sweet sentimentality; but a practical living force. Whenever we stand by the altar of incense, we become aware of the angel of the Lord standing hard by, and saying, "Fear not, O man greatly beloved ! thy prayer is heard."

When your child was a toddling, lisping babe, it asked many things wholly incompatible with your nature and its own welfare; but as the years have passed, increasing experience has moulded its requests into shapes suggested by yourself. So, as we know more of God through His promises, we are stayed from asking what He cannot give; and are led to set our hearts on things which lie on His open palm waiting to be taken by the hand of an appropriating faith. This is why all prayer, like Elijah's, should be based on promise. We stand on a foundation of adamant, and have an irresistible purchase with God, when we can put our finger on His own promise and say, "Do as Thou hast said."

(2) *It was definite.*

This is where so many prayers fail. They are shot like arrows into the air. They are like letters which require no answer, because they ask for nothing. They are like the firing by artillery in a mimic fight, when only gunpowder is employed. This is why they are so wanting in power and interest. We do not pray with any expectation of attaining definite and practical results. We wander out like Isaac to meditate in the fields at eventide: but we fail to ascend Carmel, with the compressed lip and the resolute step of Elijah; as determined, if we may, to win by prayer the fulfilment of some blessed promise, as he was to bring the longed-for rain. Let us amend in this matter. Let us keep a list of petitions, which we shall plead before God. Let us direct our prayer, as David did (Psalm v. 3), and look up for the answer; and we shall find ourselves obtaining new and unwonted blessings. Be definite !

(3) *It was earnest.*

"Elijah prayed earnestly." This is the testimony of the Holy Spirit, through the Apostle James. It was the effectual, fervent prayer of a righteous man, which availeth much. The prayers of Scripture all glow with the white heat of intensity. Remember how Jacob wrestled, and David panted and poured out his soul; the importunity of the blind beggar, and the persistency of the distracted mother; the strong crying and tears of our Lord. In each case the whole being seemed gathered up, as a stone into a catapult and hurled forth in vehement entreaty. Prayer is only answered for the glory of Christ; but it is not answered unless it be accompanied with such earnestness as will prove that the blessing sought is really needed.

Ah, what earnestness pants and throbs on every side ! No listless attention ! No flagging interest ! No drowsy eye ! Oh for such violence, guided by holiness, to take the kingdom of heaven by force ! Such earnestness is, of course, to be dreaded when we seek some lower boon for ourselves. But when, like Elijah, we seek the fulfilment of the Divine promise,—not for ourselves, but for the glory of God—then it is impossible to be too much in earnest, or too full of the energy of prayer.

(4) *Elijah's prayer was humble.*

"He cast himself down on the ground, and put his face between his knees." We scarcely recognize him, he seems so to have lost his identity. A few hours before, he stood erect as an oak of Bashan; now, he is bowed as a bulrush. Then as God's ambassador he pleaded with man; now as man's intercessor he pleads with God. Is it not always so— that the men who stand straightest in the presence of sin bow lowest in the presence of God ? And is it not also true, that those who live nearest God are the most reverent? True, thou art a child; but thou art also a subject. True, thou art a redeemed man; but thou canst never forget thine original name, *sinner.* True, thou mayest come with boldness; but remember the majesty, might, and power of God, and take thy shoes from off thy feet. The angels of His presence fly with veiled faces to do His bidding, as they cry, "Holy, Holy, Holy !" The most tender love, which cast out the fear that hath torment, begets a fear that is as delicate and sensitive as that of John; who, though he lay his head on Jesus' breast, scrupled too hastily to intrude upon the grave where He had slept. Our only plea with

God is the merit and blood of our great High Priest. It becomes us to be humble.

(5) *It was full of expectant faith.*

"Whatsoever things ye desire, when ye pray, believe that ye receive them: and ye shall have them." Faith is the indispensable condition of all true prayer. It is the gift of the Holy Ghost. It thrives by exercise. It grows strong by feeding on the promises: the Word of God is its natural food. It beat strongly in Elijah's heart. He knew that God would keep His word, and so he sent the lad— possibly the widow's son—up to the highest point of Carmel, and bade him look towards the sea; because he was sure that ere long his prayer would be answered, and God's promise would be kept. We have often prayed, and failed to look out for the blessings we have sought. The stately ships of heaven have come up to the quays, laden with the very blessings we asked; but as we have not been there to welcome and unload them, they have put out again to sea. The messenger pigeons have come back again to their cotes, with the tiny messages concealed beneath their wings; but we have not been there to search for them and take them.

Sometimes we have to exercise faith on the simple warrant of God's Word. At other times, God seems to give us special faith for things which are not directly promised. The presence or absence of faith is a great test in prayer. Where it is present, we are so sure of the answer as to turn petition into thanksgiving. But where it is persistently absent, and where continued prayer fails to light up the spirit with the conviction of coming answer, then it would seem as if the Urim and Thummim stone is darkening with one of God's loving *Noes*; and He says, "Ask me no more concerning this matter."

There is a faith which God cannot refuse; to which all things are possible; which laughs at impossibility; which can move mountains and plant them in the sea. May such faith be ours!—but it can be ours only by careful and eager nurture. Such faith was Elijah's.

(6) *It was was very persevering.*

He said to his servant, "Go up now, look toward the séa." And he went up, and looked, and said, "There is nothing." How often have we sent the lad of eager desire to scan the horizon!—and how often has he returned with the answer, *There is nothing!* There is no tear of penitence in those hard eyes. There is no symptom of amendment in that wild life. There is no sign of deliverance in these sore perplexities. There is nothing. And because there is nothing when we have just begun to pray, we leave off praying. We leave the mountain brow. We do not know that God's answer is even then upon the way.

No so with Elijah. "And he said, Go again seven times." There is a truer rendering of this: "*Then said he seven times, Go again.*" It is not that the lad was told to run to and fro seven times, without interrupting the prophet in prayer; but it would appear that again and again the lad came back to his master with the same message, "There is nothing;" and, after an interval, he was bidden to go again.

He came back the first time, saying, "There is nothing,— no sign of rain, no cloud upon the clear sky:" and Elijah said, "Go again." And that was repeated seven times. It was no small test of the prophet's endurance; but he was not tried more than he could endure, and with the ordeal there came sufficient grace, so that he was able to bear it.

Not unfrequently our Father grants our prayer, and labels the answer for us; but He keeps it back, that we may be led on to a point of intensity, which shall bless our spirits for ever, and from which we shall never recede. "But none of them that wait on Him shall be ashamed." Then when we have outdone ourselves, He lovingly turns to us, and says, "Great is thy faith: be it unto thee even as thou wilt!" He waits, that He may be gracious unto us.

(7) *And the prayer was abundantly answered.*

For weeks and months before, the sun had been gathering up from lake and river, from sea and ocean, the drops of mist, drawing them as clouds in coronets of glory around himself; and now the gale was bearing them rapidly towards the thirsty land of Israel. "Before they call I will answer, and whilst they are yet speaking I will hear." The answer to your prayers may be nearer than you think. It may already have started by the down-line. On the wings of every moment it is hastening towards you. God shall answer you, and that right early.

Presently the lad, from his tower of observation, beheld on the horizon a tiny cloud, no bigger than a man's hand, scudding across the sky. No more was needed, to convince an Oriental that rain was near. It was, and is, the certain precursor of a sudden hurricane of wind and rain. The lad was sent with an urgent message to Ahab, to descend from Carmel to his chariot in the plain beneath, lest Kishon, swollen by the rains, should stop him in his homeward career. The lad had barely time to reach the royal pavilion ere the heavens were black with clouds and wind, and there was a great rain.

The monarch started amid the pelting storm; but fleeter than his swift steeds were the feet of the prophet, energized by the hand of God. He snatched up his streaming mantle, and twisted it around his loins; and amid the fury of the elements, with which the night closed in, he outstript the chariot, and ran like a common courier before it to the entrance of Jezreel, some eighteen miles distant. He did this to convince the king that in his zeal against idolatry, he was actuated by no personal disrepect to himself, and prompted only by jealousy for God.

Thus by his faith and prayer this solitary man brought back the rain to Israel. "More things are wrought by prayer than this world wots of." Why should not we learn and practise his secret? It is certainly within the reach of us all. Then we too might bring from heaven spiritual blessings, which should make the parched places of the church and the world rejoice and blossom as the rose.

X

HOW THE MIGHTY FELL!
(1 KINGS XIX)

AMID the drenching storm with which the memorable day of the convocation closed in, the king and the prophet reached Jezreel. Probably they were the first to bring tidings of what had occurred. Elijah went to some humble lodging for shelter and food; whilst Ahab repaired to the palace where Jezebel awaited him. All day long the queen had been wondering how matters were going on Mount Carmel. She cherished the feverish hope that her priests had won the day; and when she saw the rain-clouds steal over the sky, she attributed the welcome change to some great interposition of Baal, in answer to their pleadings. May not some such colloquy as this have taken place between the royal pair, when they met in the palace-interior?—

"How have things gone to-day? No doubt, well; the rain has anticipated your favourable reply."

"I have nothing to tell you that will give you pleasure."

"Why! has anything happened?"

"The worst has happened."

"What do you mean? Where are my priests?"

"You will never see them again."

"Never see them again! What do you mean? Tell me quickly!"

"They are all dead; by this time their bodies are floating out to sea."

"Who has dared to do this thing? Did they not defend themselves? Did you not raise your hand? How did they die? Where is Elijah? Have the people broken into revolt?"

"Then Ahab told Jezebel all that Elijah had done; and withal how he had slain the prophets with the sword."

Jezebel's indignation knew no bounds. She was like a tigress robbed of her young. Ahab's temperament was sensual and materialistic; if only he had enough to eat and drink, and the horses and mules were cared for, he was content. He could not understand people becoming so enthusiastic about religious matters. In his judgment there was not much to choose between God and Baal. His was the motto of the Epicurean, "Let us eat and drink; for tomorrow we die." Not so Jezebel. She was as resolute as he was indifferent. Crafty, unscrupulous, and intriguing, she moulded Ahab to her mind; and, in doing so, anticipated the symbol of the Apocalypse, in which the scarlet-clad woman rides upon the beast.

To Jezebel the crisis was one of gravest moment. Policy as well as indignation prompted her to act at once. If this national reformation were permitted to spread, it would sweep away before it all that she had been labouring at for years. She must strike, and strike at once; and where would her blow tell so well as when aimed at the master-spirit of the day's proceedings? So that very night, amid the violence of the storm, she sent a messenger to Elijah, saying, "So let the gods do to me, and more also, if I make not thy life as the life of one of them, by to-morrow about this time." That message betrays the woman. She did not dare to kill him, though he was easily within her power; and so she mastered her wrath, and contented herself with threats. Her mind was set on driving him from the country; so that she might be left free to repair the havoc he had caused. In this, alas! she was only too successful.

Elijah's presence had never been so necessary as now. The work of destruction had commenced; and the people were in a mood to carry it through to the bitter end. The tide had turned, and was setting in towards God; and he was needed to direct its flow; to keep the people true to the choice which they had made; and to complete the work of reformation by a work of construction. From what we have seen of him, we should have expected that he would receive the message with unruffled composure; laying it before God in quiet confidence, assured that He would hide him, in the secret of His pavilion, from the wrath of man, and shield him from the strife of tongues. Surely he will preserve a dignified silence, or return an answer like that which Chrysostom sent on a similar occasion to the Empress Eudoxia. "Go tell her I fear nothing but sin." But, instead of this, we are told (and surely the sacred historian must have heaved a deep sigh as he wrote the words), "When he saw that, he arose, and went for his life."

"He went for his life!" Accompanied by his servant, and under covert of the night, he hurried through the driving storm, across the hills of Samaria; and directed his course, with true Bedouin instinct, towards the extreme south of Judæa, where the pasture lands of Palestine fade into the drear expanse of the Arabian desert. Nor did he slacken his speed till he had left far behind him the country over which Jezebel's sceptre swayed, and had reached Beersheba, the town that clustered round the well of the oath—where, centuries before, Abraham had planted a grove, and called upon the name of the Lord. He was safe there; but even there he could not stay. His spirit seems to have become utterly demoralized and panic-stricken. He could not even brook the company of his servant; so, leaving him in Beersheba, he plunged alone into that wild desert waste that stretches southwards to Sinai.

Through the weary hours he plodded on beneath the burning sun; his feet blistered by the scorching sands; no ravens, no Cherith, no Zarephath were there; no human sympathy lent him its kindly aid; the very presence of God seemed to have withdrawn itself from his side. At last the fatigue and anguish overpowered even his sinewy strength, and he cast himself beneath the slight shadow of a small shrub of juniper, and asked to die. "It is enough: now, O Lord, take away my life; for I am no better than my fathers. Let me die here and now; and bury me with Thine own hand, as Thou didst Moses in the valley of Bethpeor."

What might have been ! If only Elijah had held his ground—dwelling in the secret place of the Most High, and hiding under the shadow of the Almighty—he might have saved his country; and there would have been no necessity for the captivity and dispersion of his people. The seven thousand secret disciples would have dared to come forth from their hiding places, and avow themselves; and would have constituted a nucleus of loyal hearts, by whom Baal had been replaced by Jehovah. Yes, and his own character would have escaped a stain which has resisted the obliterating erasure of the ages, and still remains, fraught with shame and sorrow. Elijah's influence in Israel never recovered from that one false step. He missed a chance, which never came again. And though God in His mercy treated him lovingly and royally as a child, He never again re-instated him as a servant in just the position which he so thoughtlessly flung away. It is a solemn thought for us all ! If for one moment we are left to ourselves we may take a step which may shatter our influence; and for ever after put us into a very different position from that which might have been ours, if only we had remained true. As children we may be forgiven: as servants we are never reinstated, or trusted quite as we were once.

It is noteworthy that the Bible saints often fail just where we should have expected them to stand. Abraham was the father of those who believe; but his faith failed him when he went down to Egypt, and lied to Pharaoh about his wife. Moses was the meekest of men; but he missed Canaan, because he spoke unadvisedly with his lips. John was the apostle of love; yet in a moment of intolerance, he wished to call down fire out of heaven. So Elijah, who might have been supposed to be superior to all human weakness, shows himself to be indeed "a man of like passions with ourselves."

The old castle which from its hill watches over the town of Edinburgh, clustering beneath, was captured only once in the whole history of Scotland; and its capture happened thus. Its defenders thought that, on one side, the steepness of the rock made it inaccessible and impregnable; and they put no sentries there. And so, in the grey mist of the early morning, a little party crept up the precipitous slopes and surprised the garrison into surrender.

Is there not a warning here for us all? It may be that some have been saying boastfully of certain forms of vice, "I shall never yield to this or that. I have no inclination to such forms of sin. This is one of the points in which I am strong to resist." Beware!—it may be that the great enemy of souls has a special design in producing in you a sense of false security; that he may assail and vanquish you in the very point in which you deem yourself impregnable, and so forbear to watch.

What a proof is here of the veracity of the Bible! Had it been merely a human composition, its authors would have shrunk from delineating the failure of one of

its chief heroes. No artist would think of snapping a
column, just as it was tapering to its coronal. Men sometimes complain against the Bible for its uncompromising
portraitures. Yet, is not this its glory ? It holds the mirror
up to human nature, that we may learn what is in man;
that we may none of us despair; and that we may infer
that, if God were able to fashion His choicest ware out of
such common earth, it is possible for Him to do as much
again, in the most ignorant and degraded of His children.
Is there not even a gleam of comfort to be had out of the
woeful spectacle of Elijah's fall ? If it had not been for
this, we should always have thought of him as being too
far removed from us to be in any sense a model. We should
have looked on him as we do at the memorials of a race of
giants, with whom we have nothing in common. But now,
as we see him stretched under the shade of the juniper tree
asking for death, behaving himself with more pusillanimity
than many amongst us would have manifested, we feel
that he was what he was, only by the grace of God, received through faith. And by a similar faith we may
appropriate a similar grace to ennoble our mean lives.

SEVERAL CAUSES ACCOUNT FOR THIS TERRIBLE FAILURE.

(1) *His physical strength and nervous energy were completely overtaxed.*

Consider the tremendous strain which he had undergone
since leaving the shelter of the quiet home at Zarephath.
The long excitement of the convocation, the slaughter of
the priests, the intensity of his prayer, the eighteen miles
swift run in front of Ahab's chariot, succeeded by the rapid
flight, which had hardly been relaxed for a single moment,
till he cast himself upon the desert sand, had resulted in
sheer exhaustion. He was suffering keenly from reaction,

now that the extreme tension was relaxed; and this counted largely in the unutterable depression under which he was suffering.

We are "fearfully and wonderfully made;" and our inner life is very sensitive to our outward conditions. It has been truly said, that the most trivial causes—a heated room, a sunless day, want of exercise, or a northern aspect—will make all the difference between happiness and unhappiness; between faith and doubt; between courage and indecision. Many who send for the religious teacher would be wiser if they sent for their physician. And if any who read these lines are conscious of having lost the sunny gladness and buoyant faith of former days; before they speak of the mysterious hidings of God's face, or lament their own backslidings, it might be well to inquire if there may not be some physical or nervous cause. And if there be, it will attract, not the blame, but the compassionate sympathy of Him who knoweth our frame, and remembereth that we are but dust. When we consider the speed and strain of our times, it is marvellous that there are not more amongst us suffering from the intolerable depression beneath which Elijah sank on the desert sand.

(2) He was keenly sensitive to his lonely position.

"I only am left." Some men are born to loneliness. It is the penalty of true greatness. At such a time the human spirit is apt to falter, unless it is sustained by an heroic purpose, and by an unfaltering faith. The shadow of that loneliness fell dark on the spirit of our Divine Master Himself when he said: "Behold, the hour cometh, yea, is now come, that ye shall be scattered, every man to his own, and shall leave Me alone; and yet I am not alone, because the Father is with Me." If our Lord shrank in the penumbra of that great eclipse, it is not wonderful that Elijah cowered in its darksome gloom. You remind me that he might have had the company of his lad. But remember there is company which is not companionship. We may be more lonely in a crowd than in a desert. We need something more than human beings; we need human hearts, and sympathy, and love.

(3) *He looked away from God to circumstances.*

Up to that moment Elijah had been animated by a most splendid faith, because he had never lost sight of God. "He endured as seeing Him who is invisible." Faith always thrives when God occupies the whole field of vision. But when Jezebel's threats reached him, we are told most significantly, "*when he saw that*, he arose, and went for his life." In after years, Peter walked on the water until he looked from his Master to the seething waves. "*When he saw the wind boisterous* he was afraid; and, beginning to sink, he cried, Lord save me!" So here, whilst Elijah set the Lord always before his face, he did not fear, though an host encamped against him. But when he looked at his peril, he thought more of his life than of God's cause; and was afraid of man that should die, and of the son of man that should be made as grass; and forgot the Lord, his Maker, which made heaven and earth. "*When he saw that*, he arose, and went for his life."

Let us refuse to look at circumstances, though they roll before us as a Red Sea, and howl around us like a storm. Circumstances, natural impossibilities, difficulties, are nothing in the estimation of the soul that is occupied with God. They are as the small dust that settles on a scale, and is not considered in the measurement of weight. O men of God, get you up into the high mountain, from which you may obtain a good view of the glorious Land of Promise; and refuse to have your gaze diverted by men or things below!

It is a great mistake to dictate to God. Elijah wist not what he said, when he told God that he had had enough of life, and asked to die. If God had taken him at his word, he would have died under a cloud; he would never have heard the still small voice; he would never have founded the schools of the prophets; or commissioned Elisha for his work; he would never have swept up to heaven in an equipage of flame.

What a mercy it is that God does not answer all our prayers! How gracious He is in reading their inner meaning, and answering that! This, as we shall see, is what He did for His tired and querulous servant.

How many have uttered those words, " It is enough! " —the sufferer, weary of long and wearing pain; the wife tied to an inhuman husband; the Christian worker, whose efforts seem in vain: " It is enough. Let me come home. The burden is more than I can bear. The lessons are tiresome. School-life is tedious; holidays will be so welcome. I cannot see that anything will be gained by longer delay. It is enough! "

O silly, silly children! little do we know how much we should miss, if God were to do as we request. To die now would be to forego immeasurable blessings which await us within forty days' journey from this; and to die like a dog, instead of sweeping, honoured and beloved, through the open gates of heaven. It is better to leave it all in the wise and tender thought of God. He wants us home; but will not let us come till we have learnt the last lesson and done the last stroke of work. And we shall yet live to thank Him that He refused to gratify our wish, when, in a moment of despondency, we cast ourselves upon the ground, and said, " Let us die. It is enough! "

XI

LOVING-KINDNESS BETTER THAN LIFE
(1 KINGS XIX)

THE HOLY Apostle, whose earliest lessons of the love of
God were conned as he leaned on the bosom of Christ,
tells us, in words deep and simple as some translucent
lake, that " *we have known and believed the love that God
hath to us.*" They are wonderful words for mortal to
utter. A lifetime would be well spent if, at its close, we
could utter them without exaggeration. But alas! many
of us have learnt some of our deepest lessons of the love of
God, in having experienced its gentle kindness amid
shortcoming and failure, like that which marred Elijah's
course.

That failure, as we have seen, was most disastrous. It
inflicted lasting disgrace upon Elijah's reputation. It
arrested one of the most hopeful movements that ever
visited the land of Israel. It struck panic and discouragement into thousands of hearts which were beginning to
gather courage from his splendid zeal. It snapped the only
brake by which the headlong descent of Israel downwards
to destruction could have been prevented. It brought
discredit and rebuke on the cause and name of God. A
choir of angels might well have gathered around the truant
prophet as he lay upon the desert sand, and recited some
such mournful words as those with which the sweet
Psalmist lamented the death of Saul and Jonathan on
Gilboa's fatal field: " How are the mighty fallen in the
midst of battle! O man of God, thou hast tripped to thy

110

fall upon thy high places; we are distressed for thee; how are the mighty fallen; and the weapons of war perished!"

If ever it were befitting for a man to reap what he had sown, and to suffer the consequences of his own misdeeds, it would have been so in the case of Elijah. But God's thoughts are not as man's. He knew all the storms of disappointment and broken hope which were sweeping across that noble spirit, as gusts of wind across an inland sea. His eye followed with tender pity every step of His servant's flight across the hills of Samaria. He did not love him less than when he stood, elate with victory, hard by the burning sacrifice. And His love assumed, if possible, a tenderer, gentler aspect, as He stooped over him, whilst he slept. As a shepherd tracks the wandering sheep, from the fold to the wild mountain pass, where eagles, sailing in narrowing circles, watch its faltering steps—so did the love of God come upon Elijah, as, worn in body by long fatigue, and in spirit by the fierce war of passion, he lay and slept under the juniper tree.

And God did more than love him. He sought, by tender helpfulness, to heal and restore His servant's soul to its former health and joy. At His command an angel, twice over, prepared a meal upon the desert sand, and touched him, and bade him eat. No upbraiding speeches; no word of reproach; no threats of dismissal; but only sleep and food, and kindly thoughtfulness of the great journey which he was bent on making to Horeb, the mount of God. It makes us think of Him who, in after days, prepared in the early morning, upon the shore of the lake, a breakfast such as wet and weary fishermen would love— there was a fire and fish laid thereon, and bread. And He did this for those who, following the impulsive lead of Peter, had apparently determined to wait no more for His coming; but to return to the boats and fishing tackle, from which He had called them three years before.

It may be that these words will be read by those who have failed. You once avowed yourselves to be the Lord's, and lived for a little on the uplands, where the golden light ever shines upon the happy spirit; or you professed to enter the blessed life, and you did taste its joys, and experience its liberty and victory; or you have stood up to teach others, stirring them to deeds of heroic courage and daring. But all that is over now. You have fallen, as Milton's Arch-angel, from heaven to hell. We need not now discuss the cause of your failure: you were overtaken in some sudden temptation; or you neglected communion with God; or you refused to live up to your light. But the sad fact remains, that you have failed; and perhaps failed, as Elijah did, where every one expected you to stand. And you are ashamed; you want to hide yourself from all who knew you in happier days; you have given up heart and hope, and lie dejected and dispirited on the desert sands; you account yourself forsaken by God and man. But remember: though forsaken by man, you are not forgotten of God. He loves you still, and pities you, and yearns over you; and waits beside you, with loving tendance and provender, in order to restore your soul, and give you back the years that the cankerworm and caterpillar have eaten. We have then, in this incident, four thoughts of the love of God which must be a comfort to us all; and especially to those who have fallen from Carmel's height to the level of the desert sands.

I. GOD'S LOVE IN ITS CONSTANCY.

It is a fact which we all admit; but which we seldom realize in the moments of depression and darkness to which we are all exposed. It is not difficult to believe that God loves us, when we go with the multitude to the house of God, with the voice of joy and praise, and stand in the inner sunlit circle; but it is hard to believe that He feels as much love for us when, exiled by our sin to the land of Jordan and of the Hermonites, our soul is cast down within us, and deep calls to deep, as His waves and billows surge around. It is not difficult to believe that God loves us when, like Elijah at Cherith and on Carmel, we do His commandments, hearkening unto the voice of His word; but it is not so easy when, like Elijah in the desert, we lie stranded, or, as dismasted and rudderless vessels, roll in the trough of the waves. It is not difficult to believe in God's love when with Peter we stand on the mount of glory, and, in the rapture of joy, propose to share a tabernacle with Christ evermore; but it is well-nigh impossible when, with the same Apostle, we deny our Master with oaths, and are abashed by a look in which grief masters reproach.

Yet we must learn to know and believe the constancy of the love of God. We may not feel it. We may deem it shut up and gone for ever. We may imagine that we have forfeited all claim to it. We may think of it as Arctic travellers, dying in the icy darkness, dream of the summers of early childhood, which they shall never see again. But nevertheless, it has not altered; staunch as the affection of a friend; true as the love of a mother, the love of God abides unchangeable as Himself. Mists, born of the swamps and marshes of your own sin, obscure the light of that sun: but it is shining yet as brilliantly as ever; and will shine on till it has dispelled all shrouding veils, and bathes you again in its warm and blessed glow.

O man of God, lying amid the wrecks of what might have been, take heart! hope thou still in the love of God;

trust in it; yield to it; and thou shalt yet praise Him, who is the health of thy countenance and thy God.

II. GOD'S LOVE MANIFESTED IN SPECIAL TENDERNESS BECAUSE OF SPECIAL SIN.

We do not read that an angel ever appeared to Elijah at Cherith or Zarephath, or awakened him with a touch that must have been as thrilling as it was tender. Ravens, and brooklets, and a widow woman had ministered to him before; but never an angel. He had drunk of the water of Cherith; but never of water drawn by angel hands from the river of God, which is ever full of water. He had eaten of bread and flesh foraged for him by ravens, and of meal multiplied by miracle; but never of cakes moulded by angel fingers. Why these special proofs of tenderness? Certainly it was not because God took any pleasure in His servant's sin, or condoned his grave offence; but because a special manifestation of love was needed to convince the prophet that he was still dearly loved; and to soften his spirit; and to lead him to repentance.

Where ordinary methods will not avail, God will employ extraordinary ones. There is one memorable instance of this, which has afforded comfort and hope to multitudes who have sinned as Peter did, and who will bless God for ever for the record of the Master's dealings with His truant servant. The Lord sent a general message to all His disciples to meet Him in Galilee. But He felt that Peter would hardly dare to class himself with the rest; and so He sent to him a special message, saying: " Go tell My disciples, *and Peter*." It is thus that Jesus is working still throughout the circles of His disciples. So eager is He to convince the fallen of His unaltered love, that He will go out of His way to show it. He will invent new and unwonted surprises. He will employ angels with their gentle touch; and bake special cakes on desert stones. He will send special messages, entwined about the backslider's name. He will take the wandering sheep on His shoulders to bring it home, He will kill the fatted calf, and call on the angels of His presence-chamber to make merry and be glad.

It may be that you are sleeping the sleep of insensibility or of despair; but all the while the love of God is inventing some unique manifestation of its yearning tenderness. He hates your sin, as only infinite holiness can. He yearns over you as only infinite love can. He wants to convince you of what He feels; to touch you; to soften you; to win you back to Himself. All the while that you are grieving Him, and wandering from Him, He is encompassing you with blessings. Be conquered! Yield to Him! Take with you words, and turn again unto the Lord. He will receive you graciously.

III. GOD'S LOVE IN ITS UNWEARIED CARE.

It is most likely that it was evening when the angel came the first time and touched him, and bade him arise and eat; for we are told that he went *a day's journey* into the wilderness, before he sat down under the juniper bush. Night was spreading her temporary veil over the scorched sands; and the sun was sinking, like a ball of fire, on the unbroken rim of the horizon. And when the angel of the Lord came *the second time,* it would probably be as morning was breaking over the world. And thus, through the intervening night, the angels of God kept watch and ward about the sleeping prophet.

None of us can measure the powers of endurance in the love of God. It never tires. It fainteth not, neither is

weary. It does not fail, nor is it discouraged. It bears all
things; believes all things; hopes all things; endures all
things. It clings about its object with a divine tenacity,
until the darkness and wandering are succeeded by the
blessedness of former days. It watches over us during the
hours of our insensibility to its presence; touching us ever
and anon; speaking to us; and summoning us to arise to a
nobler, better life, more worthy of ourselves, more glorify-
ing to Him.

IV. GOD'S LOVE ANTICIPATING COMING NEED.

This always stands out as one of the most wonderful
passages in the prophet's history. We can understand God
giving him, instead of a long discourse, a good meal and
sleep, as the best means of recruiting his spent powers.
This is what we should have expected of One who knows
our frame and remembers that we are dust, and who pities
us as a father pitieth his children. But it is very wonderful
that God should provision His servant for the long journey
that lay before him: " Arise and eat; because the journey
is too great for thee."

That journey was undertaken at his own whim; it was
one long flight from his post of duty; it was destined to
meet with a grave remonstrance at its close: " What doest
thou here, Elijah ? " And yet the Lord graciously gave him
food, in the strength of which he could endure the long
fatigue. The explanation must be again sought in the
tender love of God. Elijah's nature was clearly over-
wrought. Without doubt he had steadfastly made up his
mind for that tedious journey to the Mount of God.
Nothing would turn him from his fixed purpose. And
therefore, as he would go, God anticipated his needs,
though they were the needs of a truant servant and a

rebellious child. In wrath He remembered mercy, and prevented him with the blessings of His goodness, and imparted, through a single meal, sufficient strength for a march of forty days and forty nights. Let us pause here for a moment to adore the wonderful love of God; which gives men life and breath and all things, even when He knows that they will be used for selfish ends, and in direct opposition to His revealed will.

Surely these thoughts of the love of God will arrest some from pursuing any longer the path of the backslider. You have failed; but do not be afraid of God, or think that He will never look on you again. In thinking thus of Him, you grieve Him more, and aggravate your ill-behaviour. Rather cast yourself upon His love, as a swimmer flings himself upon the buoyant waves, which immediately close around him, and bear him up, and carry him upon their sunlit bosom. Tell Him how deeply you mourn the past; ask Him to restore you; give yourself to Him again; resume the forsaken work; retake the abandoned post; and believe that God will again use you as a chosen vessel, and pour through you His tides of blessing, as an ocean may pour its flood through one narrow strait.

And as we close this precious narrative, may we not all receive instruction concerning those meals which Heaven prepares for us, each evening and morning, during our journey across the sands of time ? At night when we come home wearied with the day's toil, before we fling ourselves into deep slumber, the angels bid us arise and partake of that living Bread and Water, on which alone can spirits become strong. And morning by morning their gentle touches awake us from overdue slumbers, as they whisper: " Arise and eat, lest the journey be too great for thee." Their neglect to obey the heavenly summons is the true cause of so much failure in the lives of Christian people.

They do not feed enough on Christ. They slumber on, heedless and insensate, till the morning sun is high, and the angels, with their provisions, have faded away.

May we be amongst the happy number who never need twice calling; but who rise each morning, as the first cadence of the angel-voice breaks upon their ears, to eat of that flesh, which is meat indeed, and to drink of that blood, which is drink indeed. Then shall we be able to withstand all assaults; to endure all fatigue; and to abide perpetually in the realized presence of God. " They that wait upon the Lord shall renew their strength; they shall mount up with wings as eagles; they shall run and not be weary; and they shall walk and not faint."

XII

THE "STILL, SMALL VOICE"
(1 KINGS XIX)

REFRESHED by sleep and food, Elijah resumed his journey across the desert to Horeb. Perhaps no spot on earth is more associated with the manifested presence of God than that sacred mount. There the bush burned with fire; there the law was given; there Moses spent forty days and nights alone with God. It was a natural instinct that led the prophet thither, and all the world could not have furnished a more appropriate school. Natural scenery and holy associations lent all their powers to impress and elevate the soul.

Forty times the prophet saw the sun rise and set over the desert waste. I do not know that any one has perfectly explained the meaning of that symbolic number which so frequently appears upon the page of Scripture, and is so often associated with failure and temptation. In passing, I can only note the fact of its frequent repetition. Thus, at last, the prophet came to Horeb, the mount of God. We have to consider how God dealt with His dispirited and truant child.

I. GOD SPAKE TO HIM.

In some darksome cave, among those rent precipices, Elijah lodged; and, as he waited, in lonely musings, the fire burned in his soul. But he had not long to wait. "Behold, the word of the Lord came unto him."

That word had often come to him before. It had come
to him at Thisbe. It had come to him in Samaria, after he
had given his first message to Ahab. It had come to him
when Cherith was dry. It had come to summon him from
the solitudes of Zarephath to the stir of active life. And
now it found him out, and came to him again. There is
no spot on earth so lonely, no cave so deep and dark, that
the word of the Lord cannot discover and come to us.

But though God had often spoken to him before, He
had never spoken in quite the same tone—" What doest
thou here, Elijah ? " The accent was stern and reproach-
ful: " Thou art My servant; thou art set to do My will; if
ever thou wast needed, it is now; the tide is on the turn; a
great reformation is almost ripe. Why hast thou left thy
post ? How camest thou hither without My bidding or
My leave?" Elijah shrank from a direct reply. If he had
answered truly, he must have confessed that he was utterly
in the wrong, without a single word of extenuation or
excuse. He had done wrong in leaving his post; and that
first wrong step had been aggravated by every one which
he had taken since, plunging him further and further into
the dark.

If the prophet had answered that searching question of
God with shame and sorrow; if he had confessed that he
had failed, and asked for forgiveness; if he had cast himself on the pitifulness and tenderness of his Almighty
Friend—there is not the least doubt that he would have
been forgiven and restored. The past would never have
been named against him; and the results of his fatal flight
would have been repaired. God would Himself have stood
in the breach, until His child could hasten back again to
his post, and lead on the glorious work which he had so
nobly commenced. But instead of this, he parried the
Divine question, and evaded it. He did not try to explain

how he came there, or what he was doing. He chose rather
to dwell upon his own loyalty for the cause of God; and to
bring it out into striking relief by contrasting it with the
sinful backslidings of his people. " I have been very jealous
for the Lord God of Hosts: for the children of Israel have
forsaken Thy covenant; thrown down Thine altars; and
slain Thy prophets with the sword; and I, even I only, am
left, and they seek my life, to take it away." All this was
well-known to God; and I do not think the prophet would
ever have alluded to it, unless he had been hard pressed
to find an excuse to palliate his own cowardice and neglect
of duty.

In point of fact, he was thoroughly demoralized with
unbelief and fear. The sky of his soul was covered with
clouds so dense, that no star of comfort glimmered through
their murky curtains. There was a tinge of self-vindication
and of blame on others, which were scarcely worthy of him.
He did not sufficiently realize that the fault lay with himself; and that he equally with others was to blame for the
pass to which the cause of God had come. His was a noble
nature, under a temporary cloud; a palace in ruins; a
splendid vessel rolling rudderless in the trough of the waves.
There was, no doubt, truth in what he said. He was full
of zeal and holy devotion to the cause of God. He had
often mourned over the national degeneracy. He keenly
felt his own isolation and loneliness. But these were not
the reasons why at that moment he was hiding in the cave;
nor were they the real answer to that searching question,
" What doest thou here, Elijah ? "

How often is that question put still! When a Christian
worker, sorely needed, deserts his post, because of some
unforeseen difficulty, or to secure selfish gratification and
ease; to that couch of indolence, or to that forest glade
where soft breezes blow, the question comes, " What doest

thou here ? " When a child of God is found in the theatre, the dancing saloon, or the place of evil companionship; sitting in the seat of scorners, or walking in the way of the ungodly—again must the question come as a thunderbolt out of a clear sky, " What doest thou here ? " When one endowed with great faculties digs a hole in the earth, and buries the God-entrusted talent, standing idle all the day long among the loungers in the market-place, again must the inquiry ring out, " What doest thou here ? "

Life is the time for doing. The world is a great workshop, in which there is no room for drones. God Himself worketh as the great Master-builder. All creatures fulfil their needful functions, from the angel that hymns God's praise to the wasp that buries a corpse. There is plenty to do. Evil to put down; good to build up; doubters to be directed; prodigals to be won back; sinners to be sought. " What doest thou here ? " Up, Christians, leave your caves, and do! Do not do in order to be saved; but being saved, DO!

II. GOD TAUGHT HIM BY A BEAUTIFUL NATURAL PARABLE.

He was bidden to stand at the entrance to the cave; but this he hesitated to do, until afterwards. Did that hesitancy arise from a guilty conscience, reminding him that all was not right between him and God ?

Presently there was the sound of the rushing of a mighty wind; and in another moment a violent tornado was sweeping past. Nothing could withstand its fury. It rent the mountains, and broke in pieces the rocks before the Lord; the valleys were littered with splintered fragments; *but the Lord was not in the wind.* And when the wind had died away, there was an earthquake. The mountain swayed to and fro, yawning and cracking; the ground heaved as if an Almighty hand were passing beneath it; *but the Lord was not in the earthquake.* And when the earthquake was over, there was a fire. The heavens were one blaze of light, each pinnacle and peak glowed in the kindling flame; the valley beneath looked like a huge smelting-furnace; *but the Lord was not in the fire.*

How strange! Surely these were the appropriate natural symbols of the Divine presence. If we had been asked to describe it, we should have used these first of all. But hark! a still small whisper is in the air—very still, and very small, like the trembling echoes of a flute which is being played among the hills. It touched the listening heart of the prophet. If the more tumultuous outburst of power had expressed the storm and passion of his nature, this elicited and interpreted a sweeter, nobler self, and cast a softening spell over his tempest-tossed spirit, and seemed to be the tender cadence of the love and pity of God which had come in search of him. Its music drew him from the cave, into the innermost recesses of which he had been driven by the terrible convulsions of nature. " And it was so, when Elijah heard it, that he wrapped his face in his mantle, and went out, and stood in the entering in of the cave."

What was the meaning of all this ? It is not difficult to understand. Elijah was most eager that his people should be restored to their allegiance to God; and he thought that it could only be done by some striking and wonderful act. He may have often spoken thus with himself: " Those idols shall never be swept from our land, unless God sends a movement swift and irresistible as the *wind*, which hurries the clouds before it. The land can never be awakened except by a moral *earthquake*. There must be a baptism of *fire*." And when he stood on Carmel, and beheld the panic among the priests and the eagerness among the people, he thought that the time—the set time—had come. But all that died away. That was not God's chosen way of saving Israel. And because He did not go on working thus, Elijah thought that He was not working at all; and abandoned himself to the depths of despondency.

But in this natural parable God seemed to say:—" My child, thou hast been looking for Me to answer thy prayers with striking signs and wonders; and because these have not been given in a marked and permanent form, thou hast thought Me heedless and inactive. But I am not always to be found in these great visible movements; I love to work gently, softly, and unperceived; I have been working so; I am working so still; and there are in Israel, as the results of My quiet gentle ministry, ' seven thousand, all the knees which have not bowed unto Baal, and every mouth which hath not kissed him.' " Yes, and was not the gentle ministry of Elisha, succeeding the stormy career of his great predecessor, like the still small voice after the wind, the earthquake, and the fire? And is it not probable that more real good was effected by his unobtrusive life and miracles than was even wrought by the splendid deeds of Elijah?

We often fall into similar mistakes. When we wish to promote a revival, we seek to secure large crowds, much evident impression, powerful preachers; influences comparable to the wind, the earthquake, and the fire. When these are present, we account that we are secure of having the presence and power of God. But surely Nature herself rebukes us. Who hears the roll of the planets? Who can detect the falling of the dew? Whose eye has ever been injured by the breaking of the wavelets of daylight on the shores of our planet? " There is no speech, nor language; their voice is not heard." At this moment the mightiest forces are in operation around us; but there is nothing to betray their presence. And thus was it with the ministry of the Lord Jesus. He did not strive, nor cry, nor lift up, nor cause His voice to be heard in the streets. Whilst men were expecting Him at the front door, with blare of trumpet, He stepped into His destined home in the disguise of a peasant's child. His going forth is ever prepared as the morning. He comes down as showers on the mown grass. His Spirit descends as the dove, whose wings make no tremor in the still air. Let us take heart! God may not be working as we expect; but He is working. If not in the wind, yet in the zephyr. If not in the earthquake, yet in the heart-break. If not in the fire, yet in the warmth of summer. If not in thunder, yet in the still, small voice. If not in crowds, yet in lonely hearts; in silent tears; in the broken sobs of penitents; and in multitudes, who, like the seven thousand of Israel, are unknown as disciples.

But Elijah refused to be comforted. It seemed as if he could not shake off the mood in which he was ensnared. And so when God asked him the second time: " What doest thou here, Elijah ? " he answered in the self-same words, with which he had tried to justify himself before. " And he said, I have been very jealous . . ."

It is pleasant to think of those seven thousand disciples, known only to God. We are sometimes sad, as we compare the scanty number of professing Christians with the masses of ungodly. But we may take heart: there are other Christians beside. That harsh-seeming governor is a Joseph in disguise. That wealthy owner of the garden in Arimathea is a lowly follower of Jesus. That member of the Sanhedrim is a disciple; but secretly, for fear of the Jews. For every one entered on our rolls of communicants, there are hundreds—perhaps thousands—whom God shall reckon as His, when He makes up His jewels. But if you, dear reader, are one of that number, I entreat you, do not remain so: it puts you in a false position; it robs the cause of God of your help and influence; it is an act of treachery to Christ Himself. Beware lest, if you are ashamed of Him, the time may come when He shall be ashamed of you.

It is quite true that confession means martyrdom in one form or another; and sometimes our heart and flesh shrink back, in unutterable anguish, as we contemplate the possible results of refusing the act of obeisance to Baal. But at such times, let us cheer ourselves by anticipating the august moment when the dear Master will speak our names before assembled worlds, and own us as His. And let us also ask Him in us and through us to speak out and witness a good confession; effecting that in us and by us, which we are totally powerless to effect by ourselves.

We are all doing more good than we know. Elijah thought that he was doing nothing, except when battling with idolatry and sin. He never thought how often he was helping those seven thousand, by the indirect influence of his example. We, perhaps, accomplish less by our great efforts than we effect by a consistent life, a holy character, a daily shining. Lighthouse-keepers never know how many weary longing eyes turn in the darkness to the silent light they maintain through the dark night. Our duty is to shine, not asking questions, not eager for great results; but content to do the will of God, consistently, humbly, and constantly, sure that God is not unrighteous to forget our work of faith and labour of love.

XIII

"GO, RETURN!"

(1 KINGS XIX)

IT is a very solemn thought, that one sin may for ever, so far as this world is concerned, wreck our usefulness. It is not always so. Sometimes—as in the case of the Apostle Peter—the Lord graciously restores, and re-commissions for His work, the one who might have been counted unfit ever again to engage in it. "Feed my sheep. Feed my lambs." But against this one case we may put three others, in each of which it would seem as if the sentry angel, who forbade the return of our first parents to Paradise, were stationed with strict injunctions to forbid any return to the former position of noble service.

The first case is that of Moses. No other man has ever been honoured as was he, "with whom God spake face to face." The meekest of men; the servant of the Lord; the foster-nurse of the Jewish nation, whose intercessions saved them again and again from destruction. Yet, because he spake unadvisedly with his lips, and smote the rock twice, in unbelief and passion, he was compelled to bear the awful sentence: "Because ye believed Me not, to sanctify Me in the eyes of the children of Israel, therefore ye shall not bring this congregation into the land which I have given them." Most earnestly did he plead for a revocation of that terrible prohibition. But he was silenced by the solemn reply, against which there was no appeal: "Let it suffice thee; speak no more unto Me of this matter."

The second case is that of Saul, the first, ill-fated king of Israel, whose reign opened so auspiciously, as a morning without clouds; but who soon brought upon himself the sentence of deposition. Yet it was only for one single act. Alarmed at Samuel's long delay, and at the scattering of the people, he intruded rashly into a province from which he was expressly excluded, and offered the sacrifice with which the Israelites were wont to prepare for battle. "And it came to pass that, as soon as he had made an end of offering the burnt-offering, behold, Samuel came. And Samuel said, What hast thou done? . . . Thou hast done foolishly: thou hast not kept the commandment of the Lord thy God, which He commanded thee: for now would the Lord have established thy kingdom upon Israel for ever. But now thy kingdom shall not continue; . . . because thou hast not kept that which the Lord commanded thee." Thus early in his reign, and before his further disobedience in the case of the Amalekites—for that one act of disobedience, revealing, as it did, a sad state of moral decrepitude—Saul was rejected.

The third case is that of Elijah. He was never reinstated in quite the position which he had occupied before his fatal flight. True, he was bidden to return on his way, and work was indicated for him to do. But that work was the anointing of three men, who were to share amongst them the ministry which he might have fulfilled if only he had been true to his opportunities, and faithful to his God. God's work must go on; if not by us, then, through our failures, by others brought in to supply our place. "Go, return on thy way to the wilderness of Damascus: and when thou comest, anoint Hazael to be king over Syria; and Jehu the son of Nimshi shalt thou anoint to be king over Israel: and Elisha the son of Shaphat of Abel-meholah shalt thou anoint to be prophet in thy room."

Those words rang out the death-knell of Elijah's fondest dreams. Evidently, it was not for him to be the deliverer of his people from the thraldom of Baal. Others were to do his work, another was to be prophet in his room.

The terrible importance of these instances is emphasized by words which ring out with awful force amid the graceful tenderness of the parable of the Vine. "Every branch in Me," the Master said, "that beareth not fruit, He taketh away." It is impossible to suppose that these words refer to our ultimate salvation; for those same lips, not very long before, had said that His sheep should never perish, and that none should pluck them out of His hand. How, then, can it be, that the great Husbandman should ever take away the unfruitful branch? The answer is suggested at once when we consider that the drift of the teaching of that parable is not concerning our ultimate salvation, but our Christian usefulness. It is not a question as to whether we shall be saved or lost; but whether we use the opportunities given to us, and so have them continued, or forfeit them by our inattention and lethargy. If we refuse to let the Vine pour its forces through us, we shall be taken from the position of possible fruitfulness which had been entrusted to us; and the very opportunity of ministry will be withdrawn. Considerations like these should fill us with eager desire to show ourselves approved unto God, workmen not needing to be ashamed.

All those who hold prominent positions amongst us, as public teachers and leaders, may well take warning by these solemn examples standing on the plains of time, as Lot's wife on those of Sodom. We may not all be tempted, as Elijah was, to unbelief and discouragement. But there are many other snares prepared for us by our great enemy, and strewn over with fair appearances; as the hunter strews earth and grass on the top of the pitfall, which he has cunningly dug in the pathway between the river and the lair of his prey. There is the adulation given to the successful man, in which so much of the human is mingled with thankfulness for the help or comfort given. There is the desire to be always prominent—foremost on every platform, and first in every enterprise, to the utter neglect of private prayer. There are the insidious attacks of jealousy; depreciation of others; comparison of their standing with our own. And in addition to these, are other modes of failure, more gross and evident than they, to which we are all prone, and by which, alas! too many have been mastered. Any one of these may compel God to cast us away from His glorious service; employing us only in such humbler ministry, or to anoint our successors.

As children, He will never cast us away; but as His servants He may. Let us beware! One false step; one hurried desertion of our post; one act of disobedience; one outburst of passion: any one of these may lead our heavenly Father to throw us aside, as Samson did the jawbone of the ass with which he had slain heaps upon heaps. We shall not forfeit heaven; that is guaranteed to us by the precious blood of Christ. We may even be favoured by a glorious and triumphant entrance thither in an equipage of flame. But we shall never again ride on the crest of the flowing tide, carrying all before us. Others shall finish our uncompleted task.

But with the danger there are sufficient safeguards. Let God prune you with the golden pruning-knife of His holy Word. Look into the mirror of revealed truth, to see if there is any trace of blemish stealing over the face of the soul. Offer your spirit constantly to the Holy Spirit; that He may detect and reveal to you the beginnings of idolatries and heart-sins. Be very jealous of anything that divides your heart with your Lord. "Watch and pray, lest

ye enter into temptation." Have perpetual recourse for
cleansing, to the blood shed for the remission of sin. Trust
in Him who is "able to guard you from stumbling, and to
set you before the presence of His glory without blemish,
in exceeding joy."

But now, turning to the further study of the words with
which God dismissed His servant from Horeb, let us notice
three distinct thoughts.

I. The variety of God's instruments.

Hazael, king of Syria; Jehu, the rude captain; and
Elisha, the young farmer. Each was as different as possible
from the others; and yet each was needed for some special
work in connection with that idolatrous people. HAZAEL
was destined to be the rod of divine vengeance to Israel at
large; by whom God began to cut them short, and to make
them like the dust by threshing. Ah! cruel indeed was
his treatment of them! (2 Kings viii. 12; x. 32; xii. 3, 17).
JEHU was to be the scourge of the house of Ahab, extirpat-
ing it root and branch. ELISHA's ministry was to be genial
and gentle, as summer rain and evening dew; like the
ministry of our Lord Himself, whom he prefigured, and of
whom his name significantly spoke.

It is remarkable how God accomplishes His purposes
through men who only think of working their own wild
way. Their sin is not diminished or condoned because
they are executing the designs of Heaven; it still stands
out in all its malignant deformity. And yet, though they
are held accountable for the evil, it is none the less evident
that they do whatsoever God's hand and God's counsel
determined before to be done. This fact is often referred
to in Scripture. Joseph comforted his brethren, after his
father's death, by telling them that though they thought

evil against him, God meant it unto good, to save much people alive. David forbade his men to slay Shimei; because, though the cursing of the king was a foul act of treason, yet, probably, "the Lord had said unto him, Curse David." And our blessed Lord, when about to be delivered into the hands of wicked men, said that "the Father" was putting the cup into His hands (see also Acts ii. 23).

Men may do evil things against us, for which they will be condemned; and yet those very things, being permitted by the wisdom and love of God, are His messages to us. Before they can reach us, they must pass through His environing, encompassing presence; and if they do, then they are God's will for us: and we must meekly accept our Father's discipline, saying, "Not my will, but Thine be done."

II. No one can entirely escape from God's personal dealings.

God's nets are not all constructed with the same meshes. Men may escape through some of them; but they cannot escape through all. If they elude the Gospel ministry, they will be caught by some earnest worker, apt at personal dealing. If they manage to evade all contact with the living voice, they may yet be reached by the printed page. If they evade all religious literature, they may still be the sudden subjects of the strivings of the Spirit. "Him that escapeth the sword of Hazael shall Jehu slay; and him that escapeth from the sword of Jehu shall Elisha slay."

We do not read that Elisha ever wielded the sword; and yet the ministry of gentle love is sometimes more potent in slaying souls than the more vigorous ministry of an Hazael or Jehu: and out of such slaying comes life.

Let us not compare man with man. Let us not despise any sect, or denomination, or body of Christian workers. What is inoperative with one is God's voice to another. We are totally unable to estimate the essential use of men. And let us not envy one another; because each of us has some special gift which qualifies us for the use of the dear Master, and enables us to touch some who would be unreached if it were not for us. "Many members; yet but one body. And the eye cannot say unto the hand, I have no need of thee; nor again, the head to the feet, I have no need of you."

And as we look around on the entire range of ministry by which the world is filled, we may be sure that every one has at least one chance; and that God so orders the lives of men that once at least during their course they are encountered by the kind of argument which is most appropriate to their character and temperament, if only they will give ear and yield.

III. God never overlooks one of his own.

Elijah thought that he alone was left as a lover and worshipper of God. It was a great mistake. God had many hidden ones. "Yet I have left Me seven thousand in Israel, all the knees which have not bowed unto Baal, and every mouth which hath not kissed him." We know nothing of their names or history. They were probably unknown in camp or court; obscure, simple-hearted, and humble. Their only testimony was one long refusal to the solicitations of the foul rites of idolatry. They groaned and wept in secret; and spake often one to another, while the Lord hearkened and heard. But they were all known to God; and enrolled amongst His jewels; and counted as a shepherd tells his sheep. He cared for them with an infinite solicitude; and it was for their sake that He raised up the good and gentle Elisha to carry on the nurture and discipline of their souls.

It has often been a subject of wonder to me how these seven thousand secret disciples could keep so close as to be unknown by their great leader. Otto of roses will always betray its presence, hide it as we may. When salt has not lost its savour, it cannot be hid. And the work of God in human hearts must, sooner or later, discover itself. It is to be feared, therefore, that the godliness of these hidden ones was very vague and colourless, needing the eye of omniscience to detect it. But for all that, God did detect it; and He prized it. He did not quench the smoking flax; but fanned it. He did not despise the grain of mustard-seed; He watched its growth with tender love and care.

You may be very weak and insignificant—not counted in the numberings of God's captains; not deemed worthy of a name or place amongst His avowed servants: and yet, if you have but a spark of faith and love, if you strive to keep yourself untainted by the world, you will be owned by Him whose sceptre is stretched out to the most timid suppliant. But remember: if your inner life be genuine, it will not remain for ever secret—it will break out as a long-hidden fire; it will force its way into the light as the buried seed in which there is the spark of life.

It may be that God, by these lines, will speak to some backslider, saying: Go, return! Return to Me, from whom you have wandered. Return to My work, which you have deserted. Return to the posture of faith, from which you have fallen. Return to the happy, holy childlikeness of former years. "Return, ye backsliding children; and I will heal your backslidings." Oh that the response may be, "Behold, we come unto Thee; for Thou art the Lord our God!"

XIV

NABOTH'S VINEYARD
(1 KINGS XXI)

IN a room of the palace, Ahab, King of Israel, lies upon his couch, his face towards the wall, refusing to eat. What has taken place? Has disaster befallen the royal arms? Have the priests of Baal been again massacred? Is his royal consort dead? No; the soldiers are still flushed with their recent victories over Syria. The worship of Baal has quite recovered the terrible disaster of Carmel; Jezebel—resolute, crafty, cruel, and beautiful—is now standing by his side, anxiously seeking the cause of this sadness; which was, perhaps, assumed to engage her sympathy, and to secure, through her means, ends which he dared not compass for himself.

The story is soon told. Jezreel was the Windsor of Israel; and there stood the favourite residence of the royal house. On a certain occasion, whilst Ahab was engaged there in superintending his large and beautiful pleasure-grounds, his eye lighted on a neighbouring vineyard, belonging to Naboth the Jezreelite; which promised to be so valuable an addition to his property, that he resolved to procure it at all hazards. He therefore sent for Naboth, and offered, either a better vineyard in exchange, or the worth of it in money. To his surprise and indignation, Naboth refused both. And Naboth said to Ahab, "The Lord forbid it me, that I should give the inheritance of my fathers unto thee."

At first sight this refusal seems churlish and uncourteous. But a little consideration will justify the refusal of Naboth,

and aggravate the subsequent guilt of the royal pair. By
the law of Moses, Canaan was considered as being, in a
peculiar sense, God's land. The Israelites were His
tenants; and one of the conditions of their tenure was, that
they should not alienate that which fell to their lot, except
in cases of extreme necessity; and then only till the year of
Jubilee. The transfer was always coupled with the condition that the land might be redeemed at any moment,
before that time, by the payment of a stipulated price. If
these two conditions had remained in force, Naboth would
have felt less compunction at this temporary alienation of
his paternal inheritance; but both had probably fallen into
disuse, and he anticipated that if it once passed out of his
hands, his patrimony would become merged in the royal
demesne, never to be disintegrated. Taking his stand then
on religious grounds, he might well say: "The Lord forbid
it me." His refusal was in part, therefore, a religious act.

But there was, without doubt, something further. In his
mention of "the inheritance of his fathers," we have the
suggestion of another, and most natural reason, for his
reluctance; beneath those vines and trees his fathers had
for generations sat; there he had spent the sunny years of
childhood. Many a holy memory was associated with that
spot; and he felt that all the juice ever pressed from all the
vineyards in the neighbourhood, would never compensate
him for the wrench from those clustered memories.

Naboth's refusal made Ahab leap into his chariot and
drive back to Samaria; and, like a spoilt child, turn his
face to the wall in a pet, "heavy and displeased." At the
close of the previous chapter we learn that he was heavy and
displeased with God; now he is agitated by the same strong
passions towards man. In a few more days the horrid deed
of murder was perpetrated; which at one stroke removed
Naboth, his sons, and his heirs, and left the unclaimed

property to fall naturally into the royal hands. There are many lessons here, which would claim our notice, if we were dealing with the whole story; but we must pass them by, to bend our attention exclusively on the part played by Elijah amid these terrible transactions.

I. HE WAS CALLED BACK TO SERVICE.

How many years had elapsed since last the word of the Lord had come to Elijah, we do not know. Perhaps five or six. All this while he must have waited wistfully for the well-known accents of that voice, longing to hear it once again. And as the weary days, passing slowly by, prolonged his deferred hope into deep and yet deeper regret, he must have been driven to continued soul-questionings and searchings of heart; to bitter repentance for the past, and to renewed consecration for whatever service might be imposed upon him. Using a phrase employed of another, as remarkable for physical force as Elijah was for spiritual power, we may say, "the hair of his head began to grow again."

It may be that these words will be read by some, once prominent in the Christian service, who have been lately cast aside. They have been removed from the sphere they once filled. They have found audiences slip away from them, and opportunities close up. They have seen younger men step in to fill the ranks from which they have fallen. This may be attributable to the sovereignty of the Great Master—who has a perfect right to do as He will with His own, and who takes up one and lays down another. But before we lay this flattering unction to our souls, we should inquire whether the reason may not lie within our own breasts; in some inconsistency or sin, which needs confession and forgiveness at the hands of our faithful and merciful High Priest, before ever again the word of the Lord can come to us.

It is also quite possible that we are left unused for our own deeper teaching in the ways of God. Hours, and even years, of silence are full of golden opportunities for the servants of God. In such cases, our conscience does not condemn us or accost us with any sufficient reason arising from ourselves. Our simple duty, then, is to keep clean, and filled, and ready; standing on the shelf, meet for the Master's use; sure that we serve if we only stand and wait; and knowing that He will accept, and reward, the willingness for the deed. "Nevertheless, thou didst well, in that it was in thine heart."

II. ELIJAH WAS NOT DISOBEDIENT.

Once before, when his presence was urgently required, he had arisen to flee for his life. But there was no vacillation, no cowardice now. His old heroic faith had revived in him again. His spirit had regained its wonted posture in the presence of Jehovah. His nature had returned to its equipoise in the will of God. He arose, and went down to the vineyard of Naboth, and entered it, and strode through its glades, or waited at the gate, to find the royal criminal. It was nothing to him that there rode behind Ahab's chariot two ruthless captains, Jehu and Bidkar (2 Kings ix. 25). He did not for a moment consider that the woman who had threatened his life before might now take it, maddened as she was with her recent draught of human blood. All fear was but as the cobweb swinging across the garden pathway, and swept before the child rushing resolutely forward. Who does not rejoice that Elijah had such an opportunity of wiping out the dark stain of disgrace, which attached to him from the moment when he had forsaken, so faithlessly, the post of duty? His time of waiting had not been lost on him!

III. HE WAS ACTING AS AN INCARNATE CONSCIENCE.

Naboth was out of the way; and Ahab may have solaced himself, as weak people do still, with the idea that he was not his murderer. How could he be? He had been perfectly quiescent. He had simply put his face to the wall and done nothing. He did remember that Jezebel had asked him for his royal seal, to give validity to some letters which she had written in his name; but, then, how was he to know what she had written? Of course if she had given instructions for Naboth's death, it was a great pity; but it could not now be helped: and he might as well take possession of the inheritance! With such palliatives he succeeded in stilling the fragment of conscience which alone survived in his heart. And it was then that he was startled by a voice which he had not heard for years, saying, "Thus saith the Lord, Hast thou killed, and also taken possession?" *He* killed! No; it was Jezebel that had killed. Ah, it was in vain to shift the responsibility thus!" "Hast thou killed?" The prophet, guided by the Spirit of God, put the burden on the right shoulders.

Often a man, who dares not do a disgraceful act himself, calls a subordinate to his side, and says:—"Such a thing needs doing; I wish you would see to it. Use any of my appliances you will; only do not trouble me further about it—*and of course you had better not do anything wrong.*" In God's sight that man is held responsible for whatever evil is done by his tool in the execution of his commission. The blame is laid on the shoulders of the principal; and it will be more tolerable for the subordinate than for him in the Day of Judgment.

Further than that, but on the line of the same principle, if an employer of labour, by paying an inadequate and unjust wage, tempts his employees to supplement their scanty pittance by dishonest or unholy methods, he is held responsible, in the sight of Heaven, for the evil which he might have prevented, if he had not been wilfully and criminally indifferent.

It is sometimes the duty of a servant of God fearlessly to rebuke sinners who think their high position a licence to evil-doing, and a screen from rebuke. And let all such remember that acts of high-handed sin often seem at first to prosper. Naboth meekly dies; the earth sucks in his blood; the vineyard passes into the oppressor's hands; but there is One who sees and will most certainly avenge the cause of His servants. "Surely I have seen yesterday the blood of Naboth, and the blood of his sons, saith the Lord; and I will requite thee in this plat" (2 Kings ix. 26). That vengeance may tarry; for the mills of God grind slowly: but it will come, as certainly as God is God. And in the meanwhile in Naboth's vineyard stands Elijah the prophet; and in the criminal's heart stands conscience, with its scourge of small cords, weighted with jagged metal. This lesson is enforced again and again by our great dramatist, who teaches men who will not read their Bibles that sin does not pay in the end; that, however successful it may seem at first, in the end it has to reckon with an Elijah as conscience, and he always finds out the culprit; and with God as an avenger—and He never misses His mark.

IV. HE WAS HATED FOR THE TRUTH'S SAKE.

"And Ahab said to Elijah, Hast thou found me, O mine enemy?" Though the king knew it not, Elijah was his best friend; Jezebel his direst foe. But sin distorts everything. It is like the grey dawn which so obscures the most familiar objects that men mistake friends for foes, and foes for friends: as in the old story, the frenzied king of Wales slew the faithful hound that had saved his child from death. Many a time have men repeated the error of the disciples, who mistook Jesus for an evil spirit, and cried out for fear.

When Christian friends remonstrate with evil-doers, and rebuke their sins, and warn them of their doom, they are scouted, hated, and denounced as enemies. The Bible is detested, because it so clearly exposes sin and its consequences. God Himself is viewed with dislike. It cannot be otherwise. The Egyptians hated the blessed pillar of cloud. The Philistines sent away the ark of the covenant. Wounds shrink from salt. The broken bone dreads the gentle touch of the physician. The thief hates the policeman's lantern.

Let us not be surprised if we are hated. Let us even be thankful when men detest us—not for ourselves, but for the truths we speak. Let us " rejoice, and be exceeding glad." When bad men think thus of us, it is an indication that our influence is at the very antipodes to the bent and tenor of their lives. " What evil thing have I done," said a philosopher, " to make all these bad men speak well of me ? " " Blessed are ye, when men shall revile you, and persecute you, and shall say all manner of evil against you, falsely, for My sake. Rejoice, and be exceeding glad; for great is your reward in heaven; for so persecuted they the prophets which were before you."

Oh, do not turn from the surgeon's knife; or the lighthouse gleam; or the red warning light; or the deep baying of the hound—as if these were your foes. It is you that are wrong; not they. " Turn ye, turn ye! for why will ye die ? "

V. He was a true prophet.

Each of the woes which Elijah foretold came true. Ahab
postponed their fulfilment, by a partial repentance, for
some three years; but, at the end of that time, he went
back to his evil ways, and every item was literally fulfilled.
He was wounded by a chance arrow at Ramoth-gilead,
" and the blood ran out of the wound into the midst of
the chariot; " and as they washed his chariot in the foun-
tain of Samaria, the dogs licked his blood. Twenty years
after, when Jehu sent out to see, there was nothing of
Jezebel left for burial; only her skull, and feet, and palms,
escaped the voracious dogs as she lay exposed on that very
spot. The corpse of Joram, their son, was cast forth un-
buried on that same plot, at the command of Jehu, who
never forgot those memorable words. And there, in after
days, the armies of Israel were put again and again to the
rout, saturating the soil with richer fluid than ever flowed
from the crushed grapes of the vines. God is true, not
only to His promises, but to His threats.

Every word spoken by Elijah was literally fulfilled.
Jehovah put His own seal upon His servant's words. The
passing years amply vindicated him. And as we close this
tragic episode in his career, we rejoice to learn that he was
re-instated in the favour of God; and stamped again with
the Divine *imprimatur* of trustworthiness and truth.

XV

THE OLD COURAGE AGAIN
(2 KINGS I)

IN ORDER to understand the striking episode before us, we must think ourselves out of this dispensation, the main characteristic of which is gentle mercy; and we must imagine ourselves back in the age that ended at Calvary. It is very important to have a right understanding of our times. We must not judge the past ages by our own high standards of forgiveness and love, learnt in the life and death of Jesus Christ, the last and supreme revelation of God. And we must not import into our own age methods of thought and action which were once permissible and necessary, because cognate to the spirit of their times.

This lesson was once impressively taught by our Lord to His disciples. Fresh from the Transfiguration, He was on His way to the cross. For some reason He did not take the usual route along the eastern bank of the Jordan; but chose the more direct course through Samaria. Travelling thus, they had probably reached the spot, of which we are soon to speak, which was once scorched and blackened by the cinders of Ahaziah's troops. Below them, in the ravine of the hills, lay a village, to which they sent a deputation, asking for entertainment in the night which was darkening over them. But religious bigotry triumphed over natural feeling; and the request was absolutely refused. Oh, if they had known that He was about to purchase the redemption of a world; and to institute a religion, in which there should be neither Samaritan or Jew, but one great brother-

hood in Himself—they would surely have bade Him
welcome, and have pressed Him with hospitality, even
though the mighty transaction was to take place within the
limits of their hated rival, Jerusalem! "And when His
disciples James and John saw this, they said, Lord, wilt
not Thou that we command fire to come down from
heaven and consume them, even as Elias did? But He
turned and rebuked them, and said, Ye know not what
manner of spirit ye are of." It was as if He had said,
"Remember that in Me you have passed into a new
epoch; the affairs of the kingdom of heaven will be
managed on altogether different lines from those with
which you are familiar. I shall not destroy the law and
the prophets; but I am introducing a code which shall
fulfil them after a new and diviner fashion. The new
régime of mercy is already begun."

Let us clearly define to ourselves the difference in the
dispensations. This is after the Spirit of the Son, dwelling
in the bosom of the Father; that was after the spirit of the
servant, clad in ardent zeal for the glory of God. This
glows with the lambent fire of the Holy Ghost; that with
the devouring fire of destruction. The key-note of this is
salvation; of that vindication. The Old Testament brims
with striking teaching of the holiness and righteousness of
God. God, our Father, was as merciful and long suffering
then as now; and there were given many sweet glimpses of
His loving heart, which became more numerous as the ages
brought nigh the incarnation of the love of God. But men
cannot take in too many thoughts at once. Line must be
on line, precept on precept. And so each preliminary age
had some one special truth to teach; and that truth was
accentuated, and brought into prominence by special
proofs and episodes. The age of the Mosaic Law, which
shed its empire over the times of Elijah, was pre-eminently

the era in which those awful and splendid attributes of the
Divine character—God's holiness, justice, righteousness,
and severity against sin—stood out in massive prominence; as some of us, from the ancient capital of Switzerland, have seen the long line of Bernese Alps, rising above
the plain in distant and majestic splendour; cold in the
grey dawn; or flushed with the light of morn and eve. It
was only when those lessons had been completely learnt
that mankind was able to appreciate the love of God
which is in Jesus Christ our Lord.

Critics—who insensibly have caught their conceptions
of infinite love from the Gospels which they affect to
despise—find fault with the Old Testament because of its
austere tones and its severe enactments; they point out
many things inconsistent with the gentler spirit of our
times. There is nothing surprising here! It could not have
been otherwise, in a gradual unfolding of the nature and
character of God. The holy men who lived in those days
had never heard the gentle voice of the Son of Man speaking the Sermon on the Mount. They had, however, very
definite conceptions of the righteousness and holiness of
God, and His swift indignation on sin. This inspired many
of the Psalms in the hymnal of the Old Testament saints.
This stimulated them to do deeds from which our gentler
nature shrinks. But for this, Levi had never slain his
brethren, or Joshua the Canaanites; Samuel had never
hewed Agag in pieces before the Lord; and Elijah had
never presumed to slay the priests of Baal, or call down
fire from heaven to destroy the captains and their men.

And, as we read these deeds, we may well sink into quiet
self-questioning. We need not fall into the extreme of
Cromwell and his soldiers, and introduce the speech or acts
of those bygone days into our dealings with the enemies of
truth and God. But we do well to ask whether, granting

that we forego the outward manifestation, there is the same hatred of sin; the same zeal for the glory of God; the same inveterate enthusiasm for righteousness—as there was in those days of force, and decision, and unswerving righteousness.

These considerations will help us to understand the narrative that awaits us, and will relieve the character of Elijah from the charge of vindictiveness and passion; so that we can consider, without compunction, the rising up again in his breast of something of his old undaunted courage and heroic bearing.

The story is as follows: Ahaziah, the son of Ahab, had succeeded to his father's throne and his father's sins. He shrank in cowardly fear from the hardihood of the camp, and the dangers of the field; leaving Moab to rebel, without attempting its re-subjugation; and leading a self-indulgent life in his palace. But the shafts of death can find us equally in apparent security, as amid threatening dangers. He was leaning on the balustrade that fenced the flat roof of the palace, when suddenly it gave way, and he over-balanced himself, and was flung to the ground. Many are the balustrades on which we lean in hours of peril, which fail us to our hurt! When the first panic was over, the king was seized with intense longings to know how his illness would turn; and, in a strange freak, he sent messengers to one of the ancient shrines of Canaan, dedicated to Baal-zebub, the god of flies, the patron saint of medicine, who had some affinity with the Baal of his parents. This was a deliberate rejection of Jehovah; a daring choice of those ways which had brought the wrath of God on his father's house. It could not pass unnoticed; and Elijah was sent to meet his messengers, as they were speeding across the plain of Esdraelon, with the announcement of certain death:—" Thus saith Jehovah, thou shalt not come down from that bed on which thou art gone up; but shalt surely die."

The servants did not know the stranger. They may have been imported Tyrians, who had never mingled in the life of the nation; and who, therefore, were ignorant of the mighty prophet of God. Years also had probably elapsed since his last public appearance. However, they were so impressed by that commanding figure and authoritative tone, and so awed by that terrible reply, that they determined to return at once to the king. They found him lying on the divan, the raised platform, covered with cushions, to which he had been carried from the scene of his accident. And they told him the reason of their speedy return. Ahaziah must have guessed who he was that had dared to cross their path, and send him such a message. But, to make assurance surer, he asked them to describe the mysterious stranger. They replied that he was " a man of hair." Long and heavy tresses of unshorn hair hung heavily down upon his shoulders; his beard covered his breast, and mingled with the unwrought skins that formed his only dress. It was enough; the king recognized him at once, and said, " It is Elijah the Tishbite."

Two emotions now filled his heart. He wanted, in exasperation, to get Elijah in his power, to vent on him his wrath; and he, perhaps, cherished a secret hope that the lips which had announced his death might be induced to revoke it. He therefore resolved to capture him: and for that purpose sent a captain and a troop of fifty soldiers; and when they were struck down in death, another captain and his band. These men exceeded their duty; instead of simply acting as the tools and instruments of the royal will, they spoke with an unwarrantable insolence. " Thou man of God, the king hath said, Come down! " Either they did not hold him to be a prophet, or they gloried in putting the power of their master above that of Jehovah. In any case, the insult was less against Elijah than Elijah's God.

There was no personal vindictiveness in the terrible reply of the old prophet. I do not suppose for a moment he considered the indignity done to himself. I believe he was filled with consuming zeal for the glory of God, which had been trodden so rudely under foot; and which he must vindicate in the eyes of Israel. " If I be a man of God, let fire come down from heaven and consume thee and thy fifty." And in a moment the fire leaped from its scabbard, and laid the impious blasphemers low. That there was no malice in Elijah is clear from his willingness to go with the third captain, who spoke with reverence and humility. " And the angel of the Lord said, Go down with him; be not afraid of him. And Elijah went down with him unto the king."

(1) *A thought is suggested here of the meekness and gentleness of Christ.*

How wonderful it is to think that He who, by a single word, could have brought fire from heaven to destroy the bands that came to take Him in Gethsemane, left that word unspoken. He threw them on the ground for a moment, to show them how absolutely they were in His power; but He forbore to hurt one hair of their heads. It was a marvellous spectacle, which the legions of harnessed angels, who in mid-air waited for a word to bring them to His rescue, must have beheld with speechless amazement. The explanation is of course found in the fact that He was under the compulsion of a higher law—the law of His Father's will; the law of self-sacrificing love; the law of a covenant sealed before the foundation of the world.

The only fire He sought was the fire of the Holy Ghost. " I came to cast fire upon the earth; and what will I if it is already kindled." He strove not to avenge Himself, or vindicate the majesty of His nature. " He endured the contradiction of sinners against Himself." " He was led as a lamb to the slaughter; and as a sheep before her shearers is dumb, so He opened not His mouth." " When He was reviled, He reviled not again; when He suffered, He threatened not; but committed Himself to Him that judgeth righteously." Oh, matchless meekness! Oh, wondrous self-control! Oh; glorious example of the spirit of His own teaching! May grace be given to each of us, His unworthy followers, to walk in His steps, and to emulate His spirit; not calling for the fire of vengeance, but seeking the salvation of those who would do us hurt; dealing out not the fire of heaven, but those coals of fire, heaped on the head of our adversaries, which shall melt them into sweetness, and gentleness, and love.

(2) *There is also suggested here the impossibility of God ever condoning defiant and blasphemous sin.*

We have fallen on soft and degenerate days when, under false notions of charity and liberality, men are paring down their conceptions of the evil of sin, and of the holy wrath of God, which is revealed from heaven against *all* ungodliness and unrighteousness of men.

It is quite true that God yearns over men with unutterable pleading tenderness. " He is not willing that any should perish; but that all should come to repentance." As there is not a dying sparrow in the recesses of the deepest woods over whose last agonies the Almighty does not bend with sympathetic interest, and alleviating tenderness; so there is not one waif of humanity excluded from the warm zone of His infinite compassionateness and

tender pity. In every outbreak of human sin; in the lot of
every lost man and woman; over every street fight; at every
public-house doorstep; amid the blasphemous orgies of
every den of impurity and shame—that love lingers, full of
tears, and longings, and entreaties. " God so loved the
world."

And yet, side by side with this love to the sinner, there
is God's hatred to his sin. This longsuffering lasts only
so long as there is a possible hope of the transgressor
turning from his evil ways. " If he turn not, He will whet
His sword." The wrath of God against sinful men, who
have definitely elected their sin, slumbereth only; it is not
dead. It broods over them, held back by His desire to
give every one the chance of salvation. They may be
thankful therefore, that their lot has fallen in this parenthesis of mercy. But " because sentence against their evil
work is not executed speedily, therefore their hearts are
fully set in them to do evil." Yet the time of forbearance
will end at last, as the waiting did in the days of Noah.
Then fire will fall, of which the material flame that fell on
these insolent soldiers is a slight and imperfect symbol.
And it shall be discovered how bitter a thing it is to en-
counter the wrath of the Lamb, " when the Lord Jesus
shall be revealed from heaven with His mighty angels,
in flaming fire, taking vengeance on them that know not
God, and obey not the Gospel of our Lord Jesus Christ."

We need more proclamation of this side of the Gospel.
There is an alarming lack amongst us of the sense of sin.
Our vast populations are indifferent to the message of
mercy; because they have not been aroused with the
message of the holy wrath of God against sin. We need
again that one should come, in the power of Elijah, to do
the work of John the Baptist; and to prepare men by the
throes of conviction for the gentle ministry of Jesus

Christ. The crying need of our times is a deeper conviction of sin. And if this shall be ever brought about, it must be by the religious teachers being led to study the law as well as the Gospel; and to realize for themselves, as they can only do through the teaching of the Holy Spirit, the exceeding sinfulness of sin. Then when Elijah's fire of conviction has smitten human confidences low in the dust, there will be room for an Elisha to bind up broken hearts with the message of mercy.

(3) *We are also assured of Elijah's full restoration to the exercise of a glorious faith.*

In a former time, the message of Jezebel was enough to make him flee. But in this case he stood his ground, though an armed band came to capture him. It was as if he were able to repeat the familiar words without exaggeration: " Though an host should encamp against me, my heart shall not fear; though war should rise against me, in this will I be confident." And when he was bidden to go down with the third captain to the king, he did not hesitate; though it was to go through the streets of the crowded capital, and into the very palace of his foes. We are reminded of the entrance of Luther into Worms; and of the remonstrance of Ambrose to the mightiest emperor of his time. Do you ask the secret, and why he was able to stand so calmly beside the couch of the dying monarch, delivering his message, and retiring unharmed? Ah, the answer is not far to seek. He was again dwelling in the secret of the Most High, and standing in the presence of Jehovah. His faith was in lively and victorious exercise. He was able to gird himself with the panoply of God's mail, invulnerable to the darts of men and devils. And thus might he have spoken with himself, as he passed through the threatening perils of that crisis: " By Thee

have I run through a troop; and by my God have I leaped
over a wall. As for God, His way is perfect. He is a
buckler to all those that trust in Him."

Is it not beautiful to behold this glorious outburst of
the faith of Cherith, Zarephath, and Carmel? The old
man, nearing his reward, was as vigorous in this as in his
first challenge to Ahab. He bore fruit in old age, like one
of God's evergreens, which are full of sap. Glory be to
Him who restores the soul of His faltering saints; and
brings them up from the grave; and sets them again as
stars in His right hand; and deigns to use them once more
in His glorious service!

XVI

EVENSONG
(2 KINGS II)

IT WAS the cherished wish of Dr. Chalmers that there should be granted to him a Sabbatic decade, after the six decades of work, between the sixtieth and seventieth years of life, so completing its entire week. And it was surely a natural desire on the part of one who ranks amongst the foremost workers of our time. Whether or not this had been a specific desire of Elijah, in God's gracious providence it fell to his lot. And after a life full of storm and tempest it came to pass that at eventide there was light and peace, and a parenthesis of rest; as if the spirit of the world which he was about to enter were already shedding its spell over his path.

There is always something beautiful in the declining years of one who in earlier life has dared nobly and wrought successfully. Younger men gather round the veteran to whom they owe the inspiration and model of their lives; and call him " father," enwreathing his grey locks with crowns in which love is entwined with reverence. Seeds sown years before and almost forgotten, or reckoned lost, yield their golden returns. Memory rescues from the oblivion of the past many priceless records; whilst hope, standing before the thinning veil, tells of things not perfectly seen as yet, but growing on the gaze of the ripened spirit. The old force still gleams in the eye; but its rays are tempered by that tenderness for human frailty, and that deep self-knowledge, which years alone can yield. The crudities are ripened; the harshnesses are softened; the bitternesses are mellowed. Marah waters no longer forbid the thirsty lips; but an Elim invites the weary. And from those revered lips flow rivers of wise and loving counsel to the younger generations grouped around. Such a life-evening seems to have been Elijah's. He did not reach a great old age. In all likelihood he showed no signs of physical decay. His eye was not dim, nor his natural force abated. He probably betrayed his age more in the deeds he had done, and in the mellowness of his spirit, than in the infirmities of the natural man. Still there is little room for doubt that the noon of his life was well passed when he prepared himself for his final journey. And it must have been very grateful to him, as it was most fruitful of blessing to his country and to the cause of God, that there was granted a time of comparative calm at the close of his tempestuous career.

For those years of retirement were valuable, in the highest degree; both in their immediate results upon hundreds of young lives, and in their far-off results on the coming times.

I. THE WORK OF THE CLOSING YEARS OF ELIJAH'S LIFE.

His life has been called a " One-man Ministry "; and there is much in it to warrant the description. This one man was, as Elisha exclaimed, " The chariot of Israel, and the horsemen thereof." He made his age. Towering above all the men of his time, he cleft his way through the crowds of meaner souls; and withstood the onslaughts of evil; as a rock shakes off the waves that break on it into volumes of spray. By heroic exploits, and by deeds of superhuman might he strove single-handed against the tides of idolatry and sin that were sweeping over the land. In this he reminds us perpetually of Martin Luther, and of John Knox; all these men were spiritual giants by reason of their faith, which could appropriate the power of God—as the lightning-conductor can rob the thunder-cloud of its electric stores and bring them to the earth.

But though largely successful in keeping the cause of true religion from dying out, Elijah must often have realized the desirability of carrying on the work more systematically; and of leavening the country more thoroughly with the influence of devoted men. So, under Divine direction, he carefully fostered, if he did not altogether inaugurate, an institution which was a relic of former times, and known as the Schools of the Prophets. When we use the word "Prophet," we think of it as indicating a man who can foretell the future; and thus much confusion is introduced into our reading of Scripture. It includes this idea as a fragment of a larger meaning. The original word means "boiling or bubbling over;" and so a prophet was one whose heart was bubbling over with good matter, and with those Divine communications which struggled within him for utterance. He was a spiritual geyser; the mouthpiece and spokesman of God. "God spake in the Prophets." "Holy men spake as they were moved by the Holy Ghost." So these schools of the prophets were colleges, in which a number of young men gathered; their hearts open to receive, and their tongues to utter, the messages of God.

The Christian traveller among the Western Isles of Scotland will hardly fail to visit one small, bare, lone spot out amid the roll of the Atlantic waves. It is thy shore, Iona, of which I write! No natural beauties arrest the eye or enchain the interest. There is but one poor village, with its two boats, and a squalid population. Yet who can visit that low shore, and stand amid those crumbling ruins,

without intense emotion ?—since it was there that Columba
built the first Christian church to shed its gentle rays over
those benighted regions; and to shelter the young apostles
who carried the Gospel throughout the pagan kingdoms of
Northern Britain. With similar emotions should we stand
amid the ruins of Bethel, Gilgal, and Jericho; where, in his
declining years, Elijah gathered around him the flower of
the seven thousand, and educated them to receive and
transmit something of his own spiritual force and fire.
These were the missionary seminaries of the age; the
repositories of sacred truth and learning; and beneath his
influence, an Isaiah, a Hosea, an Ezekiel, may have first received impulses which have since thrilled through the world.
These young men were formed into separate companies
of fifty, in different towns. They were called " sons; " the
chief among them, like the *abbot* of a monastery, was called
" father." Clad in a simple dress, they had their food in
common; and dwelt in huts slightly made of the branches
of trees. They were well versed in the sacred books, which
they probably transcribed for circulation, and read in the
hearing of the people. They were frequently sent forth on
the errands of God's Spirit—to anoint a king; to upbraid
a high-handed sinner; or to take the part of oppressed and
injured innocence. It was, therefore, no small work for
Elijah to put these schools on so secure a basis that, when
he was gone, they might perpetuate his influence and guard
the flames which he had kindled.

II. THE ATTITUDE OF HIS SPIRIT IN ANTICIPATING HIS
TRANSLATION.

The old man clung to those young hearts, and felt that
his last days could not be better spent than in seeing them
once more; though he resolved to say nothing of his

approaching departure, or of the conspicuous honour that
was shortly to be conferred on him. Here is the humility
of true greatness! He foresaw that he was to enjoy an
exodus, which, in the whole history of the race, there had
been but one parallel. Yet he was so reticent about it
that, if he had had his way, no mortal eye would have
beheld it. Anyone less great would have let the secret
out; or have contrived to line the heights of the Jordan
with expectant crowds of witnesses. But, instead of this,
he kept the secret well locked-up within him, and tried to
dissuade Elisha from accompanying him a single step.
"Tarry thou here." Perhaps that loyal heart feared
attracting to himself, either then or afterwards, honour due
only to God.

Alas! what a rebuke is here for ourselves! The prophet's
evident desire to die alone shames us, when we remember
how eager we are to tell men, by every available medium,
of what we are doing for the Lord. There is not a talent
with which He entrusts us which we do not parade as a
matter of self-laudation. There is not a breath of success
that does not mightily puff us up. What wonder that our
Father dare not give us much marked success, or many
conspicuous spiritual endowments—lest we be tempted
further to our ruin! Oh, when shall we be free of
ourselves? Would that we could live so perpetually facing
the sun that we might never see the dark shadow of self!
"I could not see for the glory of that light." The Holy
Spirit of life alone can set us free from the law of sin and
death. Let us urge Him to hasten the performance of His
gracious office; and to give us the sweet humility of this
man, who was willing to efface himself, that men might
think only of his Master and Lord.

We are also deeply impressed by the calm tenour of the
prophet's course through those closing days. He knew

that ere many suns had set he would be standing in the light of eternity, mingling with his peers, understanding all the mysteries that had puzzled his eager spirit, and beholding the face of God; and we might have expected him to fill the preceding hours with ecstatic offices of devotion. But instead, he spent the days, as he had often spent them before, visiting the schools of the prophets, and quietly conversing with his friend, till the chariot swept him from his side. And, as we consider that spectacle, we learn that a good man should so live that he need make no extra preparation when death suddenly summons him; and that our best method of awaiting the great exchange of worlds is to go on doing the duties of daily life.

That was a wise and true reply of Wesley to the inquiry, "What would you do if you knew that you would have to die within three days?" "I should just do the work which I have already planned to do: ministering in one place; meeting my preachers in another; lodging in yet another, till the moment came that I was called to yield my spirit back to Him who gave it." When our summons comes, we should wish to be found, not in the place which sentiment or a false sense of religious propriety might suggest; but just doing the work which we have been appointed to do; and in the place where duty would demand our presence at that very hour. The workshop and the factory are as near heaven as the sanctuary; the God-given task as fair a height for ascension as Olivet or Pisgah.

III. THE AFFECTIONATE LOVE WITH WHICH ELIJAH WAS REGARDED.

It strongly showed itself in Elisha. The younger man stood with his revered leader, as for the last time he surveyed from the heights of Western Gilgal the scene of his former ministry. And, in spite of many persuasives to the contrary, he went with him down the steep descent to Bethel and Jericho. He followed him even though they had to cross the Jordan, which means death and judgment. The sacred historian accentuates the strength of their affection, as he says thrice over, *they two* went on; *they two* stood by Jordan; *they two* went over. And again the strength of that love, which the cold waters of death could not extinguish, approved itself in the repeated asseveration: "As the Lord liveth, and as thy soul liveth, I will not leave thee." It is sweet to think that there were in the rugged strong nature of Elijah such winsome qualities as could elicit so deep and tenacious an affection. We catch a glimpse of a tenderer side, for which we had hardly given him credit.

Unusual emotion also welled up in the hearts of the young men, whose reverence shared the empire with their love, as they beheld their master for the last time. With delicate reticence they would not speak on a subject which he did not mention; but drawing Elisha aside, they asked him whether the moment of separation had not come. "Yes," said he in effect, "but do not speak of it. Let there be no parting scene. Give and receive the parting farewells in expressive silence." And thus the old man tore himself away from them.

But in all their intercourse, how real and near the Lord seemed! To Elijah it was the Lord who was sending him from place to place: "the Lord hath sent me." To Elisha, it was the living Lord to whom he constantly appealed: "as the Lord thy God liveth"—living on the other side of the great change through which his master was to pass to Him. To the prophets, it was the Lord who was taking their head and leader to Himself. Surely those who speak thus have reached a position in which they can meet death without a tremor. And what is death but, as we shall see in our next chapter, a translation !

What is the Lord to thee, my reader ? Is He a dear and familiar friend, of whom thou canst speak with unwavering confidence ? Then thou needst not fear to tread the verge of Jordan. Otherwise, it becomes thee to get to His precious blood, and to wash thy garments white; that thou mayest have right to the tree of life, and mayest enter in through the gates into the city.

XVII

THE TRANSLATION
(2 KINGS II)

WE have reached at length one of the sublimest scenes of Old Testament story. We should have been glad to learn the most minute particulars concerning it; but the historian contents himself with the simplest statements. Just one or two broad, strong outlines; and all is told that we may know. The veil of distance, or the elevation of the hills, was enough to hide the receding figures of the prophets from the eager gaze of the group that watched them from the neighbourhood of Jericho. And the dazzling glory of the celestial cortege made the only spectator unable to scrutinise it too narrowly. What wonder, then, if the narrative is given in three brief sentences! "They still went on, and talked; and it came to pass that there appeared a chariot of fire, and horses of fire, and parted them both asunder; and Elijah went up by a whirlwind into heaven."

But there was one symptom, at least, of the coming wonder, which was clearly witnessed by more than the solitary companion who had so faithfully and tenaciously kept Elijah's side. The two friends halted for a moment before the broad waters of the Jordan, which threatened to bar their onward steps; and then Elijah's spirit was thrilled with the old omnipotent faith; such as had so often enabled him to overcome the working of natural laws, by the introduction of the laws of that higher sphere which only answer the summons of a mighty faith.

True, he took off his well-worn mantle, and wrapped it together, and smote the waters. But that, at the best, was only an outward and significant sign. At that same moment, his spirit was grappling the power of the Infinite God, and was bringing it to bear on the hurrying stream. He knew that the Lord had sent him thither, and that his road lay further into the country on the other side. He saw no means of pursuing the God-marked path. He was sure that, since his way led through the waters, God was prepared to make it possible and easy for him to tread it. And, therefore, he dared to strike the waters, believing that Divine power was working in every stroke; and the waters parted hither and thither, leaving a clear passage, through which they went.

Child of God, your path seems sometimes to lie right through a flowing Jordan. There is no alternative but that you should go straight on. Forward moves the cloud. Forward points the sign-post of circumstance. Forward bids the inward prompting. But how, when Jordan rolls in front ? Now is the time for faith ! Where God's finger points, there God's hand will make the way. Believe that it shall be so ! Advance in unfaltering faith ! Step down the shelving bank, and the waters of difficulty shall part before you; and you shall find a pathway where to human vision there was none. So through parting Jordans you shall march to your reward.

I. The Fitness of this Translation.

There was fitness *in the place*. Not the smiling plain of Esdraelon, with its cornfields and vineyards, and dotted hamlets, speaking of the toils and homes of men. Not the desert of Sinai, so closely allied with the memory of his fatal fall. Not the schools of Gilgal, Bethel, or Jericho.

None of these would furnish a fit setting for his farewell to his earthly ministry. But, away from all these; amid the scenery familiar to his early life; in view of localities for ever associated with the most memorable events of his nation's history; surrounded by the lonely grandeur of some rocky gorge—*there* God chose to send His chariot to fetch him home.

There was fitness *in the method*. He had himself been as the whirlwind, that falls suddenly on the unsuspecting world, and sweeps all before it in its impetuous course, leaving devastation and ruin in its track. It was meet that a whirlwind-man should sweep to heaven in the very element of his life. His character was well depicted in the panorama of the desert, with its shivering wind, and its glowing fire. And nothing could be more appropriate than that the stormy energy of his career should be set forth in the rush of the whirlwind; and the intensity of his spirit by the fire that flashed in the harnessed seraphim. What a contrast to the gentle upward motion of the ascending Saviour !

There was fitness *in the exclamation* with which Elisha bade him farewell. He cried, "My father, my father ! the chariot of Israel and the horsemen thereof !" Doubtless, amid that sudden flash of glory he hardly wist what he said. Yet he closely hit the truth. That man, whom he had come to love as a father, had indeed been as an armed chariot of defence to Israel. By his faith, and prayers, and deeds, he had often warded off evil and danger with more certain success than could have been effected by an armed troop. Alas that such men are rare ! But in our time we have known them; and when they have been suddenly swept from our side, we have felt as if the Church had been deprived of one main source of security and help.

II. THE REASONS FOR THIS TRANSLATION.

(1) One of the chief reasons was, no doubt, *as a witness to his times.* The men of his day were plunged in sensuality, and had little thought of the hereafter. At the very best, the Jews had but vague notions of the other life; and those notions were probably still further darkened by the obscuring influences of idolatry and sin. But here a convincing evidence was given that there was a spiritual world into which the righteous entered; and that, when the body sank in death, the spirit did not share its fate, but entered into a state of being in which its noblest instincts found their befitting environment and home—fire to fire; spirit to spirit; the man of God to God.

A similar testimony was given to the men of his time by the rapture of Enoch before the Flood; and by the ascension of our Lord from the brow of Olivet. Where did these three wondrous journeys end, unless there was a bourne which was their befitting terminus and goal? And as the tidings spread, thrilling all listeners with mysterious awe; and as they heard that no sign of the rapt ones could be discovered by the most diligent search—would there not break upon them the conviction that they likewise would have to take that wondrous journey into the unseen, soaring beyond all worlds, or sinking into the bottomless pit?

(2) Another reason was evidently the desire on the part of God *to give a striking sanction to His servant's words.* How easy was it for the men of that time to evade the force of Elijah's ministry, by asserting that he was an enthusiast, an alarmist, a firebrand! It would be convenient for them to think that his denunciations and threats began and finished with himself—the workings of a distempered brain. And if he had passed away in decrepit old age, they would

have been still further encouraged in their impious con-
jecturings. How would they have known that he spake the
truth of God ? But the mouths of blasphemers and gain-
sayers were stopped, when God put such a conspicuous
seal upon His servant's ministry. It was as if Jehovah had
stepped out of the unseen to vindicate him; and to affirm
that he was His chosen ambassador; and that the word in
his lips was true. The translation was to the life-work of
Elijah what the resurrection was to that of Jesus—it was
God's irrefragable testimony to the world.

As a servant, Elijah had failed in one fatal moment; and
by that moment's failure had missed a splendid chance : but
for all that, the general tenour of his ministry was such
as God could approve; and concerning it He could bear
His sanctioning testimony to men. It may sometimes happen that our Father will greatly honour His servants in the
eyes of men, whilst He will be very strict in His private
dealings with them in reference to certain failures in duty
of which only He and they are aware.

III. THE LESSONS OF THIS TRANSLATION FOR OURSELVES.

(1) *Let us take care not to dictate to God.* This was the
man who lay down upon the ground, and asked to die. If
he had had his will, he would have had the desert sands for
his shroud, and the desert winds for his requiem. How
good it was of God to refuse him the answer he craved !
Was it not better to pass away, missed and beloved, in the
chariot which his Father had sent for him, and with which
Ahab's, though he had run before it, could bear no comparison ?

This is no doubt one reason why our prayers go un-
answered. We know not what we ask. We ask for things
which we would not dream of, if we only knew the infinite

superiority of the lot which our Father has planned out for us. We shall have to bless Him for ever, more for the prayers He refused than for those He granted. When next your request is denied, reflect that it may be because God is preparing something for you as much better than your request as the translation of Elijah was better than his own petition for himself.

(2) *Let us learn what death is.* It is simply a translation: not a state, but an act; not a condition, but a passage. We pass through a doorway; we cross a bridge of smiles; we flash from the dark into the light. There is no interval of unconsciousness, no parenthesis of suspended animation. "Absent from the body," we are instantly "present with the Lord." Oh, do not think of death as the gaoler of a prison-house, in which he is collecting the saints against some final order for their liberty. It is nothing of the sort. It is but the grim disguise of one of the angels of God's presence-chamber, specially commissioned to bring faithful souls into the audience-room of the King. As by the single act of birth we entered into this lower life, so by the single act—which men call death, but which angels call birth (for Christ is the Firstborn from among the dead)—we pass into the real life. The fact that Elijah appeared on the Trans-figuration Mount in holy converse with Moses and with Christ proves that the blessed dead are really the living ones, sentient, active, intensely in earnest; and they entered that life in a single moment, the moment of death. Would it not be truer to speak of them not as the dead, but as those who have died, and are alive for ever. It must be remembered, however, that while it is far better for the emanci-pated soul and spirit to be with Christ, present with the Lord—the blessedness will not be complete until the resurrection of the body, which will then have put on incorruption and immortality.

(3) *Let us see here a type of the rapture of the saints.*
We do not know what change passed over the mortal
body of the ascending prophet. This is all we know, that
"mortality was swallowed up of life." There was wrought
on him a change like that which took place in the grave of
Joseph, when the crucified body of Jesus became transformed into the risen body—which was largely independent
of the laws of nature, but which was so like the body which
He had worn for thirty-three years that it was readily and
universally recognized. Corruption put on incorruption.
The mortal put on immortality. The body of humiliation
was exchanged for the body of glory.

Such a change, unless Christ tarry longer than the term
of our natural life, shall be the portion of many who read
these lines—"caught up to meet the Lord in the air." It
becomes us then to walk as Elijah did, with alert and watch-
ful spirit; talking only on themes that would not be
inconsistent with an instantaneous flash into the presence of
God. Thus, whenever our Father's carriage comes for us;
and wherever it overtakes us—whether in the storm at
sea, or in the railway accident; in the tumult of a catastro-
phe, or in the gradual decay of prolonged illness—may we
be prepared to step in, and "sweep through the gates,
washed in the blood of the Lamb !"

Was it not some reference to this august event that was
in the mind of the great Welsh preacher, Christmas Evans,
who, when dying, majestically waved his hand to the
bystanders, and looked upward with a smile, and uttered
these last words, "*Drive on !*" "The chariots of God are
twenty thousand." May we not suppose that one awaits
each departing spirit, standing ready at hand to convey it
into the presence of the King, to whom be glory for ever
and ever !

XVIII

A Double Portion of Elijah's Spirit
(2 Kings ii)

THERE is one incident for ever associated with the translation of Elijah; which, though it largely concerns his friend and successor, is so characteristic of the great prophet himself that we must not pass it over without some notice. It is deeply significant. We are told that, after they had passed the Jordan, the two friends *went on and talked.* What sublime themes must have engaged them, standing as they did on the very confines of heaven, and in the vestibule of eternity! The apostasy of Israel and its approaching doom; the ministry just closing, with its solemn warnings; the outlook towards the work upon which Elisha was preparing to enter—these and cognate subjects must have occupied them.

It was in the course of this conversation that "Elijah said unto Elisha, Ask what I shall do for thee, before I be taken away from thee." It was a very wide door flung open by the elder to his younger friend. And, at first, we are surprised to think that Elijah could offer to supply anything for which Elisha asked. Is not this rather the prerogative of God? Surely God alone can do whatsoever we desire when we pray; and even He is limited by the fulfilment, on our part, of certain essential conditions. But we must remember that Elijah was intimately familiar with the mind and heart of his brother. It was not in vain that they had spent those years of ministry together. It was with the object of testing the spirit of his friend that the departing seer had urged him again and again to leave him. And it was only when Elisha had stood the test with such unwavering resolution that Elijah was able to give him this *carte blanche*. He knew that that faithful soul would ask nothing for which he could not exercise his mighty faith, or which God could not, and would not bestow. He was only "a man of like passions with ourselves"; cast in the ordinary mould of human nature: but, by close and intimate communion with God, he had reached such a pitch of holy boldness that the very keys of spiritual blessing seemed put into his hand, so that he might dispense to kindred spirits the priceless gifts of God. Why should not we strive after and attain "like precious faith"?

I. ELISHA'S LARGE REQUEST.

Elijah's confidence was not misplaced. Elisha's reply wrought along those lines which he had anticipated. He sought neither wealth, nor position, nor worldly power; nor a share in those advantages on which he had turned his back for ever when he said farewell to home, and friends, and worldly prospects. "And Elisha said, I pray thee, let a double portion of thy spirit be upon me."

What did Elisha mean by this request? I do not interpret his request to mean that he should have twice as much of the faith and spiritual force as characterized his master. What he intended was to ask that he might be considered as Elijah's eldest son; the heir to his spirit; the successor to his work. There is a passage in the law of Moses which clearly proves that "the double portion" was the right of the firstborn and heir (Deut. xxi. 17). This the prophet sought; and this he certainly obtained.

It was a noble request! He was evidently called to succeed to Elijah's work; but he felt that he dare not undertake its responsibilities, or face its inevitable perils, unless he were specially equipped with spiritual power. It is not often that we can count an Elijah among our friends; but when we may, we shall do well to invoke his intercessions on our behalf—that we may be endowed with a similar spirit. And there is at least One to whom we can all go with this sublime request, sure that He is more eager to give us His Holy Spirit than the tenderest earthly father to satisfy his children's hunger with bread. Oh for this spiritual hunger, insatiable for the best gifts ! Men of the world hunger for name, and rank, and wealth; and they get what they seek because they will take no Nay. Blessed should we be if we were as eager after the Spirit of God; and if, instead of giving up opportunities of usefulness because we did not feel qualified to fill them, we rather sought and received a new baptism of power, a fresh endowment of the Holy Spirit.

Who need shrink from attempting Elijah's work, if first he have received Elijah's spirit ? Instead of relinquishing a work for which you do not feel naturally qualified, wait in the fervency of entreaty, and in the expectancy of faith, until you are endued with power from on high. There is no work to which God calls you for which He is not prepared to qualify you. Let it never be forgotten that Elijah himself did what he did, not by inherent qualities, but because through faith he had received such copious bestowments of the Spirit of God; and what he did we may do again—the weakest and humblest may do—if only we are prepared to wait, and watch, and pray, until our Pentecost breaks upon us with or without its sound of rushing wind, and its tongues of flaming fire.

II. LET US CLEARLY UNDERSTAND THE TWO CONDITIONS IMPOSED ON ELISHA.

(1) *Tenacity of purpose.*

Elijah tested it severely at every step of that farewell journey. Repeatedly he said, "Tarry here." But he might as well have tried to uproot a cedar of Lebanon, or to stir Carmel from its base. Neither Gilgal, with its panoramic scenery; nor Bethel, with its memories of the angel-haunted dream; nor Jericho, the border-town—was able to attract or retain him. And though their course lay through the Jordan-flood of death, it sufficed not to deter that eager spirit. Elisha knew what he sought; he read the meaning of the discipline to which he was being exposed; and his heroic resolution grew with the ordeal, as the waters of a stream grow against an arresting dam, until they overleap it and rush forward on their way. It was thus that the Syro-Phœnician woman prevailed with Christ. It was thus that the Apostles waited for the promise of the Father, undaunted by ten days' delay.

Before giving us the Holy Ghost, our Father will certainly try us, to see if we can live without Him. If we can, we may. And it is only when we give signs of a resolution which will take no denial, but detains the Angel with its imperative importunity, and vows its unalterable determination to be blessed—it is only then that God, who had never been really reluctant, and had only been testing us, turns to us with a smile, and says, "O child, great is thy importunity; be it unto thee even as thou wilt." "The kingdom of heaven suffereth violence; and the violent take it by force."

How often we persuade ourselves that we can acquire the greatest spiritual blessings without paying the equivalent piice ! Thus James and John thought that they could obtain a seat each on the throne for the asking. They did not realize that the cross preceded the crown; and that the bitter cup of Gethsemane lay between them and the coronation anthem. We must pass through the Jordan; daily must we take up the cross and follow Jesus; we must be conformed to Him in the likeness of His death, and in the fellowship of His sufferings; the old nature must be crucified; the Divine will must be lovingly accepted, though it cost tears of blood and bitter sorrow. Then, having evinced the steadfastness of our purpose, we shall approve ourselves worthy to be the recipients of God's supreme gift.

(2) *Spiritual insight.*

"If thou see me when I am taken from thee, it shall be so unto thee; but if not, it shall not be so." There was nothing arbitrary in this demand. And it would have been hardly possible to have devised a more complete criterion of the spiritual conditions of this eager aspirant. To see the transactions of the spirit-world requires a spirit of no ordinary purity, and of no ordinary faith. No mere mortal eye could have beheld that fiery cortege. To senses dulled with passion, or blinded by materialism, the space occupied by the flaming seraphim would have seemed devoid of any special interest, and bare as the rest of the surrounding scenery. Perhaps there was not another individual in all Israel with heart pure enough, or spiritual nature keen enough, to have been sensible of that glorious visitation. Had we been there, we should probably have been unconscious of anything, save the sudden disappearance of the prophet. But since Elisha saw it all, it is clear that his passions were under control; his temper refined; his spiritual life in healthy exercise; and his whole being of such an order, as to admit him into the foremost rank of the spiritual world, without risk. Such must we be, by the grace of God, ere we can aspire to possess or wield similar powers. Our reception of the Spirit will be in exact proportion to the subjection of the flesh, and the consequent vigour of our inner life.

III. THE ANSWER.

"He took up also the mantle of Elijah that fell from him." Ah, that falling mantle ! How much it meant ! It is said that the bestowal of the mantle has always been considered by Eastern people an indispensable part of consecration to a sacred office. When, therefore, Elijah's mantle fluttered to Elisha's feet, he knew at once that Heaven itself had ratified his request. He knew that he had Elijah's post. He believed that he was anointed with Elijah's power. I do not for a moment think that there was any emotional or sensible indication of the mighty change which had been wrought upon him. His spirit was still. There was no tremor in his pulse; no thrill of consciously added power in his frame. The torrent of spiritual force had entered him as quietly as light enters the world, and as the forces of spring thrill through the woods.

If, in patience and faith, we claim of our Father the filling of the Holy Ghost, we must never ask ourselves *if we feel full*. We must believe that God has kept His word with us, and that we are filled, though no celestial sign accompanies the entering glory of that power "which works effectually in them that believe." But others will become aware of the presence of something that we never had before, as they see us stand by some tameless Jordan, and behold the turbulent waters part hither and thither before our stroke.

Directly we receive some great spiritual endowment, we may expect to have it tested. It was so with Elisha. "He went back, and stood by the bank of Jordan." Did he hesitate? If so, it was but for a moment. He had seen Elijah go; and he believed, though probably he did not feel, that therefore the double portion of his spirit had fallen to his lot. He, therefore, acted upon the assurance of his faith. "He took the mantle of Elijah that fell from him, and smote the waters, and said, Where is the Lord God of Elijah? and when he also had smitten the waters, they parted hither and thither: and Elisha went over. And when the sons of the prophets which were to view at Jericho saw him, they said, The Spirit of Elijah doth rest on Elisha."

As soon as Jesus had been annointed with the Holy Ghost, He was led into the wilderness to be tempted. The title " Son of God," uttered over the waters of baptism, was made the subject of Satan's wildest attacks: " If Thou be the Son of God . . ." So must it be ever. But difficulty, temptation, and trial, avail to bring into greater prominence, both for ourselves and others, the reality and glory of the blessing we have received. The parted Jordan proves the presence of the Spirit.

" Where is the Lord God of Elijah? " That cry has often been raised when the Church, bereft of its leaders, has stood face to face with some great and apparently insuperable difficulty. And sometimes there has been more of despair than hope in the cry. But though Elijah goes, Elijah's God remains. He takes His weary workers home; but He is careful to supply their place, and to anoint others to carry on their work. It is His work, not ours. On Him is the responsibility, as to Him shall be the glory. If you ask where He is, an answer close behind you whispers, " I am here." Catch up the mantle of the departed. Emulate their lives. Seek their spirit. Smite the bitter waves of difficulty in unwavering faith: and you shall find that the Lord God of Elijah will do as much for you as for the saints who have been swept to their reward, and are now mingling with the great cloud of witnesses that are watching your conflicts, your triumphs, and your joys.

XIX

THE TRANSFIGURATION
(LUKE IX)

WORDSWORTH and all his followers were students in the school of Jesus Christ. Never breathed a more enthusiastic lover of Nature than our Lord. Lilies could not grow at His feet, or birds wing their homeward flight over His head, without attracting His swift attention. His daily talk was of wandering sheep and whitening corn; of living wells and summer rain; of the changing hues of morn and eve. We cannot wonder therefore at His snatching brief opportunities for communion with the scenes of natural beauty; or that He often climbed the everlasting hills—the natural altars of the world—obviously intended not for habitation, but for worship.

Such an occasion is the one referred to here. Wearied with His toils, and requiring time for private intercourse with His friends, to prepare them for the approaching tragedy of which they were strangely unconscious, He travelled northwards with His disciples, avoiding the larger towns, until they reached one of the smaller villages, nestling on the lower slopes of Mount Hermon, which towers into the clouds, and forms a majestic barrier on the northern frontier of Palestine. There they seem to have rested for about a week. Think how they may have spent those days! Watching the snows on the upper peaks flush in the dawn; and glow in the sunset, as if aflame. Revelling in the fertility, which centuries before had been compared to the fragrant oil, anointing the high priest. Visiting the

ancient forest of cedars, from which Hiram's servants had
hewn the beams of Solomon's temple; or the mountain
springs, where the familiar Jordan had its source. A week
would quickly pass amid engagements such as these,
blended as they must have been with intercourse on the
loftiest themes.

After eight days, Jesus took with Him His three mighties
—Peter, James, and John; and as the evening shadows
darkened over the world, He led them up to some neighbouring summit, removed from the sight and sound of
men. He went to brace Himself for the coming conflict
by prayer; and perhaps for the earlier part of the night the
favoured three bore Him fellowship. But they soon grew
weary; and presently, as afterwards in Gethsemane, were
wrapt in heavy sleep—though dimly conscious of their
Master's presence, as He poured out His soul with strong
cryings and tears. We know not how many hours elapsed
ere they were suddenly startled from their slumbers—not
by the gentle touch of morning light; but beneath the
stroke of the unbearable glory, which streamed from their
Master's person. The fashion of His countenance was
altered; the deep lines of care that had seamed it were
obliterated; the look of pensive sadness was gone. " His
face did shine as the sun "; not lit up as that of Moses was
by reflection from without; but illumined from within, as
if the hidden glory of Shekinah, too long concealed, were
bursting through the frail veil of flesh, kindling it to radi-
ance as it passed. " His raiment "—the common homespun
of the country—" became white and dazzling "; more
resplendent than the glistening snow above; and as though
angels had woven it of light. But perhaps the greatest
marvel of all was the presence of the august pair, " which
were Moses and Elijah; who appeared in glory, and spake
of His decease [His exodus—out of death into new

and resurrection life] which He should accomplish at
Jerusalem."

I. CONSIDER THE PROBABLE REASONS WHY THESE TWO,
AND ESPECIALLY ELIJAH, WERE CHOSEN ON THIS SUBLIME
OCCASION.

*The first reason might have been that they should attest
the dignity of the Lord Jesus.* He was approaching the
darkest hour of His career, when His sun should set in an
ocean of ignominy and shame; and it seemed as if heaven
itself were astir, by embassy, or delegation, or deputation,
to assure His friends, and to convince the world, of His
intrinsic worth. Should seraphs be commissioned? Nay;
for men unable to realize their rank, would be simply
dazzled. Better far to send back some of the human
family, who had passed into the unseen, but whose illustrious deeds still lived in the memory of mankind, giving
weight to their witness. Yet who should be selected?

There might have been a fitness in sending the first
Adam to attest the supreme dignity of the second; or
Abraham, the father of them that believe. But their claims
were waived in favour of these two, who might have more
weight with the men of that time, as representing the two
great departments of Jewish thought and Scripture: Moses
the founder of the Law; Elijah the greatest of the Prophets.

It is impossible to exaggerate the prominence given to
Elijah in the Jewish mind. At the circumcision of a child,
a seat was always placed for him; and at the annual
celebration of the Passover in each home, wine was placed
for him to drink—the cup for which, among richer Jews,
was made of gold, set with jewels. And it was universally
believed that he was to come again to announce the advent
of the Messiah. It would, therefore, have great weight

with these disciples, and through them with after-ages, to feel that he had stood beside Jesus of Nazareth offering Him homage and help. And it was partly the memory of the allegiance rendered by Elijah to his Master that led Peter to say, in after years, that he had been an eye-witness of His majesty.

Astronomers tell us that our sun, with its attendant worlds, is only a satellite of some other mightier star; and that these wondrous orbs are circling round some far-distant centre, known as Alcyone. If this be so, and if our mighty sun is only a satellite, what must be the glories of the central body, whose majestic progress it attends! And if Elijah were so illustrious, what must be the glories of that wondrous Being to whom he was only a servant amongst many!

Another reason may be found in the peculiar circumstances under which they left the world. Moses died, not by disease, or by natural decay, but beneath the kiss of God. His spirit passed painlessly and mysteriously to glory; whilst God buried his body. Elijah did not die. Disease and old age had nothing to do in taking down the fabric of his being. He did not sleep; but he was " changed in a moment, in the twinkling of an eye." We may not penetrate into the secrets of that mysterious border-land, which these two passed and repassed, in their holy ministry to the Saviour's spirit; but we feel that there was something in the method of their departure from our world which made that passage easier.

Yet another reason is suggested in the evident fulfilment of their ministry. They had been originally sent to prepare for Christ. " We have found Him," said Philip, " of whom Moses in the law and the prophets did write." " Moses," said Jesus, " wrote of Me." " The testimony of Jesus is the spirit of prophecy." But the Jews were in danger of forgetting this; and of attaching more importance to the messengers than was justifiable. They clung to the stars, even when the sun was steadily climbing up the sky. It was the death-warrant of Stephen, that he seemed to them to slight the Old Testament, by hinting that it would be abrogated and superseded by the New. Peter himself was quite prepared to treat Moses and Elijah on an equality with his Master, by building three tabernacles—one for each. This could not be; and therefore Moses and Elijah were swept away by a cloud, and " Jesus only " was left; and the voice of God was heard insisting that Peter and the two other disciples should listen to Him alone. It was as though God had said—uttering words that lifted a dispensation from its hinges—" As ye have listened to the Law and the Prophets, so now listen to My Son. Do not put yourselves again under the law, or rest content with the prophets, however lofty their ideals and burning their words; but give to Him all the veneration and attention that you have been hitherto wont to reserve for them. Pass from the anticipation to the reality; from the type to the perfect fulfilment. They are taken; but all that made them helpful is left."

We too must sometimes climb transfiguration mounts, and see our beloved caught away from our gaze and then return towards an unkindly and wrangling world; but let us remember that our hearts are bereft of their supports, to drive us to find all and more than all in Jesus. He is enough for any heart, however lonely and desolate. He suffices for heaven, and surely He can for earth. All that is good in any one was first in Him, and remains in Him for ever without alloy. And as one after another is caught away, we are still rich with unsearchable wealth; we are still able to cope with all the devils that await us in the vales beneath, though we have " no man save Jesus only."

Such may have been some of the reasons that led to the appearance of these two men on the Transfiguration Mount: standing there for a moment, and then receding into the land of glory from which they came; attesting His dignity, and then withdrawing—that the interest excited by their presence might not be focussed on themselves; but turned at once and more intensely on the person of Jesus Christ.

II. CONSIDER THE THEME ON WHICH THEY SPOKE.

They spoke not of the latest tidings of heaven; nor of their own wondrous past; nor of the distant future: but of the decease (lit. *the exodus*) which He was to accomplish so soon at Jerusalem.

Great men love great thoughts. And where could there have been found greater subjects than this wondrous death, and His glorious resurrection ?—which were to affect all worlds, and to involve the Son of God in shame and sorrow so unfathomable. Herein Moses and Elijah precede the greatest thinkers of mankind—Galileo, Kepler, Newton, Milton, Faraday, who have sought in the Gospel of the Cross the sea-room needed by their leviathan intellects.

Heaven was full of this theme. Angels, forsaking all other interests, were absorbed in wonder, awe, and love, as they watched each step towards the destined goal. May we not imagine all the life of heaven arrested and pausing before that stupendous tragedy ? It was natural, then, that these latest comers from those shores should talk of the one all-engrossing topic in the land which they had left.

Their own salvation depended on the issue of that wondrous death. If ever there were men who might have

stood a chance of being accepted on their own merits,
surely these were such. But they would have been most
particular in disclaiming any such distinction. Looking
back on their careers, they were deeply sensible of their
imperfections and their sins. Moses remembered the
petulance of Massah. Elijah recalled the faithlessness and
fretfulness of the desert. And, in the light of eternity, they
saw evil in many things which had seemed passably good
in the twilight of earth. They had no merits of their own.
Their only hope of salvation lay where ours does—in His
overcoming the sharpness of death, and opening the
kingdom of heaven to all believers.

And surely our Lord would lead them to dwell on a
theme so constantly present to His mind. He had always
anticipated the hour of His death. It was for this that He
had been born. But now it seemed very near. He stood
within the shadow of the cross. And it must have been
grateful to Him to talk with these lofty spirits of the
various aspects of the joy that was set before Him. Moses
might remind Him that if, as God's Lamb, He must die,
yet as God's Lamb He would redeem countless myriads.
Elijah might dwell on the glory that would accrue to the
Father. These thoughts were familiar enough to the mind
of our blessed Master; yet they must have gladdened and
strengthened Him, as they fell from other lips. The more
so, when they conversed together on the certain splendour
of the resurrection morning that should follow His decease.

*Let us learn how men view the work of Christ in the light
of eternity.*

They do not dwell primarily on the mystery of the holy
incarnation; or on the philanthropy of His life; or on the
insight of His teachings. All these things are dwarfed by
comparison with His death. That is His masterpiece—the

Mont Blanc of the glorious range of His achievements in our mortal flesh. Here the attributes of God find their most complete and most harmonious exemplification. Here the problem of human sin and salvation are met and solved. Here the travail of Creation meets with its answer and key. Here are sown the seeds of the new heavens and earth, in which shall dwell righteousness and peace. Here is the point of unity between all ages, all dispensations, all beings, all worlds. Here blend men and angels; departed spirits and the denizens of other spheres; Peter, James, and John, with Moses and Elijah: and all with the great God Himself, whose voice is heard falling in benediction from the opened heaven.

The nearer we get to the Cross, and the more we meditate on the decease accomplished at Jerusalem, the closer we shall come into the centre of things; the deeper will be our harmony with ourselves, and all other noble spirits, and God himself. Climb that mountain often, in holy reverie; and remember that in all the universe there is no spirit more deeply interested in the mysteries and meaning of our Saviour's death than that noble prophet who now seeks no higher honour than to stand for ever as near to the beloved Master, as he did, for one brief space, on the Transfiguration Mount.

XX

"FILLED WITH THE HOLY GHOST"
(LUKE i. 15, 17)

WHAT may not one man do in one brief life, if he is willing
to be simply a living conduit-pipe through which the power
of God may descend to men? There is no limit to the
possible usefulness of such a life. There, on the one hand,
is the oceanic fullness of God; here, on the other, are the
awful need and desolation of man, guilty, weak, bankrupt,
diseased: all that is required is a channel of communication
between the two; and when that channel is made and
opened, and kept free from the silting sand, there will
ensue one great, plenteous, and equable flow of power
carrying the fullness of God to the weary emptiness of
man. Why shouldest thou not be such a channel, my
reader?

There is a splendid illustration of this in the life of Elijah,
of which we are now taking our farewell. For more than
a hundred years the tide had been running strongly against
the truth of God. Idolatry had passed from the worship of
Jeroboam's calves to that of Baal and Astarte; with the
licentious orgies and hideous rites which gathered around
the ancient worship of the forces of Nature. The system
was maintained by an immense organization of wily
priests, who had settled down upon the national life like a
fungus growth, striking its roots into the heart. The court
was in its favour. The throne was occupied by an effeminate man, the weak tool of his unscrupulous and beautiful
wife—the Lady Macbeth of Jewish history. Jehovah's

184

altars were thrown down; His prophets silenced and in hiding; His faithful worshippers a mere handful, whose existence was so secret as to be known only to Him. The lamp of truth had been overturned; and there was only a tiny spark of light feebly burning, to show where once the light of true religion brightly shone.

Into such a state of things Elijah came, unarmed, from his native trans-Jordanic hills; a highlander, unkempt, unpolished; unaccustomed to the manners of a court, or the learning of the schools. Withal a man weak where we are weak; tempted where we are tempted; of like passions with ourselves. And at once the tide began to turn. The progress of idolatry received a decisive check. The existence and power of Jehovah were vindicated. New courage was infused into the timid remnant of true-hearted disciples. Altars were rebuilt; colleges were opened for the training of the godly youth; a successor was appointed; and an impetus given to the cause of truth, which was felt for many generations.

Perhaps the greatest tribute to Elijah's power with his contemporaries is in the fact that his name and work stood out in bold and clear outline for nine hundred years after his death; surpassing the whole school of Jewish prophets, as the Jungfrau rears her snow-clad peaks above the giants of her chain; and furnishing a model with which to set forth the power and courage of the forerunner of our Lord. The Holy Spirit, speaking in Malachi, the last of the prophets, could find no better symbol of the pioneer of the Christ than to compare him with the famous prophet who, centuries before, had swept to heaven in the chariot of flame: " Behold, I will send you Elijah the prophet before the great and terrible day of the Lord come." The bright angel Gabriel, standing four hundred years after amid the ascending incense of the holy place, found no easier method of conveying to the aged priest the type of the wondrous son that was to gladden his old age, than to liken him to Elijah. " He shall go before His face in the spirit and power of Elijah."

Whenever a notable religious movement was stirring through the land, the people were accustomed to think that the prophet of Carmel had again returned to earth; and thus the deputation asked John the Baptist, saying, " Art thou Elijah ? " and when a mightier than John had set all men musing in their hearts, as the disciples told our Lord, many of the common people believed that the long expectation of centuries was realized, and that Elijah was risen again. It was commonly believed that no other of woman born was great enough to precede the Messiah; and that he would anticipate His advent by an interval of three days, during which he should proclaim, in a voice heard over all the earth—peace, happiness, and salvation.

All these things are evidences of the towering greatness of Elijah's character and work. With all the failures and mistakes to which such natures are prone, he was a great man, and did a noble work. And the secret of all was to be found, not in any intrinsic qualities, but in the fact that he was filled with the Holy Ghost. Let us pause here, and ask ourselves if we can give our thoughtful assent to this statement. If we cannot, we must count much of our time and labour in these chapters wasted; for our one aim has been to establish this point. But if we can, then, as we close these chapters of stirring, sacred biography, we may resolve that we will never rest until we too are filled with the Holy Ghost. We will not rest satisfied in being imitators merely; but we will seek to be filled with the same Spirit, that He may work again through us the marvels of the past.

If I may venture so to put it, God is in extremity for

men who, thoughtless for themselves, will desire only to be receivers and channels of His power. He will take young men and women, old men and children, servants and hand-maidens, in the waning days of this era, and will fill them with the selfsame Spirit whose power was once reserved for a favoured few. Besides all this, the positive command has never been repealed which bids us be "filled with the Spirit" (Eph. v. 18). And we cannot reiterate too often that those who feel themselves bound to strict temperance in respect to wine by the former clause, should feel the latter one to be equally imperative. Moreover, what God commands, He is prepared to do all that is needful on His side to effect. Then when, like John the Baptist, we are filled with the Holy Ghost, like John the Baptist we shall go " before His face in the spirit and power of Elijah; to turn the hearts of the fathers to the children, and the disobedient to walk in the wisdom of the just; to make ready for the Lord a people prepared for Him."

I. THIS FILLING OF THE HOLY GHOST WAS THE CHARAC-TERISTIC OF THE CHURCH.

On the day of Pentecost they were *all* filled with the Holy Ghost—women as well as men; obscure disciples as well as illustrious apostles; and to guard against the leakage which is, alas! too common to us all, they were filled and filled again; those who are described as filled in Acts ii. 4, are spoken of as filled again in Acts iv. 31. New converts, like Saul of Tarsus, were bidden to expect this blessed filling. Deacons called to do the secular business of the Church must be men filled with the Holy Ghost. That he was a good man, full of the Holy Ghost, was a greater recommendation of Barnabas than that he had parted with his lands. And even churches, like those in the highlands of Galatia, were no sooner brought into existence by the labours of the Apostle Paul than they were filled with the Holy Ghost. In point of fact, the Christians of the first age were taught to expect this blessed filling. And the early Church was a collection of Holy-Ghost-filled people. Probably it was the exception, rather than the rule, *not* to be filled with the blessed presence of God the Holy Ghost.

There is no formal conclusion to the Acts of the Apostles; because God meant the story to be prolonged, through the ages, after the same manner. Let us not think that God resembles some who put a portico of marble to a building which they finish with common brick. He did not give at Pentecost an experience which He either would not or could not maintain. Pentecost was simply meant to be the specimen and type of all the days of all the years of the present age. And if our times seem to have fallen far below this blessed level, it is not because of any failure on God's part; but because the Church has neglected this holy doctrine. Christians have seemed to suppose that the filling of the Holy Ghost was the prerogative of a few; the majority of them have never thought of it as within their reach; and the Church has been simply paralysed for want of the only power that can avail her in her conflict against the world—a power which was distinctly pledged to her by her ascending Lord. We never can regain or hold our true position until all believers see that the filling of the Holy Ghost is equally for them as for the first Christians; and that the barriers are broken down which once limited it to a few. We do not seek the sound of rushing wind; or the coronet of flame; or the special gifts which were conferred for a special purpose: these are the minor accessories of this filling, with which we can dispense. But what we cannot dispense with, and must not dream of missing, is—the distinct filling of the Holy Ghost. No doubt He is in us if we are Christians; but we must never be content until He is in us in power—not a breath; but a mighty wind: not a rill; but a torrent: not an influence; but a mighty, energizing Person.

II. WE MUST COMPLY WITH CERTAIN CONDITIONS, IF WE WOULD BE FILLED.

(1) *We must desire to be filled for the glory of God.* A lady told me lately that she had long been seeking the power of the Spirit, but in vain. She could not understand the cause of her failure, till she came to see that she was seeking Him for the joy that He would bring, rather than for the glory that would accrue to God. Ah, we must seek for the Spirit's power, not for our happiness or comfort, nor yet for the good that we may be the better able to effect; but that " Christ may be magnified in our bodies, whether by life or death."

(2) *We must bring cleansed vessels.* God will not deposit His most precious gift in unclean receptacles. And we need cleansing in the precious blood, ere we can presume to expect that God will give us what we seek. We cannot expect to be free from indwelling sin; but we may at least be washed in the blood of Christ from all conscious filthiness and stain.

(3) *We must be prepared to let the Holy Spirit do as He will with and through us.* There must be no reserve; no holding back; no contrariety of purpose. The whole nature must be unbarred, and every part yielded. There is a law in physics that forces work in the direction of least

resistance. Let us present no resistance whatever to the working of the Holy Ghost. He who resists least will possess most. God gives the Holy Ghost to them that obey Him (Acts v. 32).

(4) *We must appropriate Him by faith.*—There is no need for us to wait ten days, because the Holy Spirit *has been given* to the church. This is included in the spiritual blessings with which our Father *hath* blessed us in Christ Jesus. We need not struggle, and agonize, and convulse ourselves in the vehemence of entreaty; we have simply to take what God has allotted to us, and is waiting to impart. Open your mouth wide, and He will fill it. Dig the ditches; and though you can discern no evidences of the entering floods, they shall be filled. Ask as a little child asks for its breakfast already on the table. So soon as you ask, you do receive, though you experience no rush of transcendent joy; go your way reckoning yourself filled, whether you feel so or not: and as the days go on, you will find that you have been filled, and are being filled, with new power, and joy, and wealth. You will not long be left to the reckoning of faith; for you will be made aware of a virtue going out from you, which shall heal and save.

III. TIME WOULD FAIL TO ENUMERATE ALL THE BLESSINGS THAT WILL ENSUE.

The presence of the Holy Ghost in the heart, in all His glorious fullness, cannot be hid. It will surely betray itself, as the presence of the ever-burning fire in the hot-house is indicated by the luxuriance of flower and fruit within its tropical enclosure, whilst frost and snow reign in the world without. There will be no effort; no striving after great effect; no ostentatious show. He distils as the dew upon the tender herb; and descends as the summer showers upon the mown grass. This conception of His work is clearly taught by the word selected by the Apostle to describe the results of His indwelling. He speaks of them as the "*fruit* of the Spirit," in contrast to the "*works* of the flesh*"; and what deep suggestions of quiet growth, and exquisite beauty, and spontaneousness of life lie in that significant phrase!

In passing, we can do no more than enumerate some of the results of the indwelling of the Holy Ghost.

There is victory over sin. The law of the Spirit of life in Christ Jesus makes us free from the law of sin and death; just as the law of the elasticity of the air makes the bird free from the predominating power of the down-pull of gravitation.

There is the indwelling of the Lord Jesus. Christ dwells in the heart by the Holy Ghost; so that there are not two indwellings, but one. And this not figurative or metaphorical, but a literal and glorious reality.

There is the quickening of the mortal body. An expression which certainly points to the Resurrection; but which may mean some special strength and health imparted to our present mortal bodies—the tabernacles and temples of His indwelling.

There are all the graces of the Spirit, which come with linked hands; so that it is impossible to admit one of the golden sisterhood without her introducing all the radiant band. Love brings joy; and joy peace; and peace long-suffering; and similarly through the whole series: so that the heart becomes at length tenanted, as was the grave of Christ, with angels.

There is also power for service. No longer timid and frightened, the Apostles give their witness with great power. The Gospel comes in power and demonstration through consecrated lips and lives. The very devils are exorcised; and great crowds are brought to the feet of Christ.

This and much more is awaiting the moment in thy life, my reader, when thou shalt definitely avail thyself of thy privilege and become filled with the Holy Ghost. Then as time rolls on, thou shalt work great deliverances among men, careless of praise or blame. Perhaps thou shalt know what it is to pass upward to meet Christ in the air. But certainly thou shalt stand beside Him in the regeneration when He shall appear in glory. And then in all the radiant throng there shall be nought to divert thy gaze from "Jesus only"; or thy thought from the decease (the exodus) which He accomplished at Jerusalem.

And amid the myriads of stars that shall shine for ever in the firmament of heaven, not one shall sparkle with more brilliant or more steady glory than Elijah; a man of like passions with ourselves, who through faith subdued kingdoms, wrought righteousness, obtained promises, out of weakness was made strong, waxed valiant in fight, swept to heaven unhurt by death, and stood beside Christ on the Transfiguration Mount. Prophet of Fire, till then, Farewell!